columbinus

by
the United States Theatre Project

Written by
STEPHEN KARAM and PJ PAPARELLI
Dramaturgy by
PATRICIA HERSCH
Conceived by
PJ PAPARELLI

Dramatic Publishing
Woodstock, Illinois • England • Australia • New Zealand

IMPORTANT BILLING AND CREDIT REQUIREMENTS

All producers of the play must provide the following credit in all programs distributed in connection with performances of the play and in all instances in which the title of the play appears for purposes of advertising, publicizing or otherwise exploiting the play and/or a production: "*columbinus*, by the United States Theatre project, written by Stephen Karam and PJ Paparelli, dramaturgy by Patricia Hersch, conceived by PJ Paparelli." This credit *must* also appear on a separate line, on which no other name appears, immediately following the title, and must appear in size of type not less than fifty percent the size of the title type. Biographical information on Stephen Karam, PJ Paparelli and Patricia Hersch, if included in the playbook, may be used in all programs. In all programs this notice must appear:

In addition, all producers of the play must include the following acknowledgment on the title page of all programs distributed in connection with performances of the play and on all advertising and promotional materials:

"*columbinus* had a co-world premiere on March 8, 2005,
at Round House Theatre, Silver Spring, Md. (Jerry Whiddon,
Producing Artistic Director, and Ira Hillman,
Managing Director), and then on May 6, 2005, at Perseverance
Theatre in Juneau, Alaska, (PJ Paparelli, Artistic Director,
and Jeffrey Herrmann, Producing Director)
in conjunction with the United States Theatre Project.
Originally produced in New York by
New York Theatre Workshop."

IMPORTANT PRODUCTION NOTE

The text of *columbinus* makes reference to several songs. Producers are hereby cautioned that permission to produce the Play *does not* include permission to use *any* of this material in production. Producers must procure permission to use this material from the copyright owners; or other songs, arrangements and recordings in the public domain substituted.

FOREWORD

My memory of the Columbine shootings is vague. I was immersed in a theatre production at the time that somehow disconnected me from the outside world. A pain in my tooth took me out of the insular theatre world I was in and forced me into the banality of a dentist's waiting room. I was sitting there, bored, wanting to go back to rehearsal, when I picked up a copy of *Time* magazine. On the cover were the faces of teenagers: some were victims, some their killers. I couldn't move. I was overwhelmed with disbelief. How could two teenagers do something so horrific? And why did it take me a week to realize what had happened? Three years later, I decided that never again would my mode of artistic expression not be directly connected to the world around me. I desperately wanted to create theatre events that would examine the major human events that impact our culture. The United States Theatre Project was my answer to that, and the first venture would be a search for answers to the questions of Columbine.

columbinus is not a play; it is a theatrical discussion. Its creators, a group of multi-generational artists, wanted to create a fictional world of adolescence, born out of our collective experience. Just as this fictional high school could be anywhere in America, so could the potential for a school shooting. We quickly realized that we needed to talk with this generation of adolescents and hear what they had to say about their world. At the same time, we needed to dive deep into the heart of Columbine and hear from the people who experienced the shootings, as well as teenagers living in Littleton today. We collected as much oral and written fact about Columbine as we could gather. The merger of these two worlds would be the subject for discussion.

I always thought this piece would be an answer to the notorious question: "Why?" After traveling to Littleton and meeting parents, children, survivors and community leaders, I realized there were many answers from every perspective, including from the shooters themselves. With all these answers, I noticed things had not changed even in Littleton. Life went on. And all the reasons "why" remain. I asked myself, "What could this piece suggest as a different means of prevention?" I was afraid that we would never find an answer.

I eventually answered that question with more questions: How do we treat each other? Why do we treat each other the way we do? Why do kids, who will soon ask these questions about their kids, continue to treat each other the same way? Why does this cycle never change, even after the kids themselves resort to bombs and guns and butchering their fellow students to prove a point? Why do we look for an easy answer—a pill to take, a program to turn off—when we know in our hearts that something deep inside us has to change? What are we afraid of?

The project is the definition of collaboration. Hundreds of people were involved in its creation: the people of Littleton who let us into their lives, specifically, Randy, Judy and Brooks Brown, and Frank Earley and the students of Arapahoe High School; Gerald Freedman and the North Carolina School of the Arts for their support in the early workshops; Donald Hicken and the 2003 senior company of the Baltimore School for the Arts for "telling us like it is"; the Virginia Schools: Brenda Scott and the drama students at J.E.B. Stuart and Carol Cadby and the drama students at Yorktown for allowing us to ask and being brave enough to answer; the Youth Ministry of All Saints Episcopal in Atlanta, Georgia, for their openness; Bryan Tallevi and Chris Till for their professional advice; Molly Smith and Arena Stage for letting the play be first heard; Chip Walton and Curious Theatre in Denver for letting it be heard in Denver; the Kennedy Center for letting the play be first seen; and the bravest souls: Jerry Whiddon at Round House Theatre in Washington, my incredible staff at Perseverance Theatre in Juneau, Alaska, and Jim Nicola at New York Theatre Workshop, all of whom gave the play life and an audience. Special thanks to a group of young actors who guided us in the early days: Anna, Alexis, Jordan, Adam, Ashley, Stacy, Tom and Trevor, most of whom were high school seniors when Columbine occurred. Our deepest respect and admiration go to the incredible talent and commitment of the original cast, who have forever shaped this piece: Anne, Jimmy, Ekatrina, Jeanne, Daniel and Gene. And of course, Karl and Will—Will and Karl—who carried the burden of two lost souls for four years and sacrificed and shared so much in bringing them to life. Finally, to Stephen Karam, my partner in all things Columbine, who always made me laugh and inspired me to be a better person.

columbinus is dedicated to all the voices that were silenced by the shootings on April 20, 1999. No one should ever feel that alone again.

PJ Paparelli
United States Theatre Project
May 1, 2006

columbinus had its co-world premiere on March 8, 2005, at Round House Theatre in Silver Spring, Maryland (Jerry Whiddon, Producing Artistic Director, Ira Hillman, Managing Director), and then on May 6, 2005, at Perseverance Theatre in Juneau, Alaska (PJ Paparelli, Artistic Director, Jeffrey Herrmann, Producing Director), in conjunction with the United States Theatre Project. The following artistic team collaborated on the co-world premiere:

Anne Bowles	*Faith*
Jeanne Dillon	*Perfect*
James Flanagan	*AP*
Daniel Frith	*Prep*
Gene Gillette	*Jock*
Karl Miller	*Freak / Eric Harris*
Ekatrina Oleksa	*Rebel*
Will Rogers	*Loner / Dylan Klebold*

by the United States Theatre Project
Written by Stephen Karam and PJ Paparelli
Dramaturgy Patricia Hersch
Conceived and Directed by PJ Paparelli

Additional Contributors	Josh Barrett, Sean McNall, Karl Miller, Michael Milligan, Will Rogers
Set Design	Tony Cisek
Lighting Design	Dan Covey
Sound Design	Martin Desjardins
Costume Design	Denise Umland
Projection Design	JJ Kaczynski
Stage Manager	Shawn Dean
Assistant Director	Sarah Denhardt
Associate Lighting Design	Klyph Stanford
Director of Production	Danisha Crosby

columbinus had its New York premiere on May 22, 2006, at New York Theatre Workshop (Jim Nicola, Artistic Director; Lynn Moffat, Managing Director). The following artistic team collaborated on the New York premiere:

Anna Camp	*Perfect*
James Flanagan	*AP*
Carmen Herlihy	*Rebel*
Nicole Lowrance	*Faith*
Karl Miller	*Freak / Eric Harris*
Joaquin Perez-Campbell	*Jock*
Will Rogers	*Loner / Dylan Klebold*
Bobby Steggert	*Prep*

by the United States Theatre Project
Written by Stephen Karam and PJ Paparelli
Dramaturgy Patricia Hersch
Conceived and Directed by PJ Paparelli

Additional Contributors	Josh Barrett, Sean McNall, Karl Miller, Michael Milligan Will Rogers
Scenic Design	Tony Cisek
Costume Design	Miranda Hoffman
Lighting Design	Dan Covey
Sound Design	Martin Desjardins
Projection Design	JJ Kaczynski
Production Stage Manager	Amy McCraney
Associate Lighting Design	Klyph Stanford

columbinus

A Play in Two Acts

CHARACTERS

Freak / Eric Harris
Loner / Dylan Klebold

The following characters play everyone else:

MEN	WOMEN
AP (Advanced Placement)	Faith
Jock	Perfect
Prep	Rebel

Note: The characters' names should not be listed in the program. From the audience perspective, they are simply a group of teenagers.

TIME & PLACE

From a fictional high school in suburban America to Littleton, Colorado, days prior to and including April 20, 1999.

SCENES

Scene titles should be projected at the top of each scene.

<u>ACT ONE</u>

MORNING RITUAL	PHYSICAL EDUCATION
SELECTION	HISTORY LESSON
IDENTITY	WORK
GUIDANCE: PART I	I.M. (Instant Message)
CAFETERIA	MISCHIEF
DRAMA	DINNER
CREATIVE WRITING	ALONE
GUIDANCE: PART II	

<u>ACT TWO</u>

DYLAN & ERIC
JUVENILE DIVERSION
THE BASEMENT TAPES
WHAT IF
THE PARENTS
911
THE LIBRARY
GOODBYE
AFTERMATH

ACT I

(As the audience enters, houselights and stagelights are up. The space is stark and exposed. The stage floor evokes a gymnasium. On the back wall is a giant, functional chalk slate, which can also have images or words projected onto it. There are eight school chairs and two tables.

The actors enter the space carrying their first act costumes and props. They prepare the space, then gather downstage and address the audience.)

ACTORS. Good evening (afternoon).

ACTOR (Freak). The story we will share this evening (afternoon) is based on true events, and inspired by actual people, writings and records.

ACTOR (Rebel). The characters were created from interviews and conversations with teenagers from across the country.

ACTOR (Loner). We appreciate you coming to the theatre tonight, and if you have a cell phone...now would be a great time to turn it off.

ACTORS. Thank you.

(An actor writes on the slate: COLUMBINUS. In their own time, the actors remove their clothes and strip down

to their undergarments, throwing their clothes offstage.
They lie down throughout the space, except for the AC-
TOR PLAYING LONER. He goes to lie down, then hesi-
tates. He stares at the audience as the lights fade to
black.)

MORNING RITUAL

(Alarm clocks ring. In unison, the actors swing their
arms round to the floor with a thud, silencing the bell.

MOTHER'S VOICE (Faith) *(pre-recorded)*. Rise and
   shine, sleepyhead.
FATHER'S VOICE (AP) *(pre-recorded)*. Hey, get up, get
   out of bed.
MOTHER'S VOICE. Get up...
LONER. Get out...
FATHER & MOTHER. Get up.
LONER. I'm dead...
FATHER & MOTHER. Get up. Wake up. Wake up.
ALL *("I'm" overlaps with the final "wake")*. I'm up!

   (Lights up. Everyone attempts to stay asleep.)

MOTHER You're late.
LONER. Huh?
FATHER. ...gotta run.
LONER. Huh?
FATHER & MOTHER You're late, gotta' run, run 'n go,
   see ya soon, don't be late, hey be safe, love ya bye.
LONER. I...
MOTHER. Bye.

LONER. I…
FATHER. Bye.
LONER. Good…
ALL *(sufficiently annoyed)*. Goodbye!

(Sound of door slam. Blackout. Actors sigh and bitch a bit. An alarm clock rings, and then everyone in unison smacks the floor. Lights up.)

FREAK *(rolling out of bed)*. Roll outta…
FAITH. Jump outta…
REBEL. Crawl outta…
PERFECT. Whatta wear?
JOCK *(simultaneous with "wear")*. Where's a towel?
PREP. Now'll shower.
LONER. Sour breath…
REBEL. And knots of frizzy hair.
AP. First I pee…
JOCK. Then I piss.
PREP. Lookin' good.
JOCK. Morning wood.
REBEL. First I'm thirsty.
PERFECT. First we need a…
ALL. Shower.
FREAK. I need a very, very cold shower.
LONER. I took a shower last night.
ALL *(as if saying "Yeah, right")*. Right.

(The rhythm stops. Actors sing a contemporary song while washing themselves, getting more and more exaggerated until they suddenly stop and step out of the shower into the following actions:)

PREP. Dry it.
JOCK. Shave it.
AP. Comb it.
PERFECT. Pluck it.
FAITH. Brush it.
REBEL. Let it.
FREAK. Scrub it.
LONER *(putting on his hat)*. Fuck it.
BOYS. Slick it down.
GIRLS. Put it up.
LONER. My pants are where...?

(They "discover" their costumes, behind them.)

ALL. Oh!
REBEL *(looking at her pants)*. They're wide.
FAITH. They're snug.
REBEL. They hide.
PERFECT. They low-ride.
AP. No time.
ALL. Move fast.
PREP. Flat front.
REBEL. Fat ass.
JOCK. Same old.
FREAK. Cargo.
PREP. Polo.
FREAK. Cargo.
PREP. Polo:
ALL. Button, Button, Button-fly.
FAITH & PERFECT. Wanna cry.
LONER/PREP *(exchanging shirts from across the room)*. I
   hate this shirt!

PERFECT. Skort.
FAITH. Or skirt.
PERFECT. Or short, short shorts…
PERFECT/FAITH. Or…
JOCK, FREAK, LONER, REBEL. T-shirt.
AP, PREP. A 'n F.
JOCK. F-'n A…
AP, PREP. Button-down fits well.
JOCK. …it smells. I smell.
REBEL, FREAK, LONER. Just black.
FREAK & AP. Backpack.
FAITH *(overlapping with "pack")*. Pack lunch.
PREP. Hang on a sec.
AP. A quick e-mail check.
REBEL & PREP. I strap it on.
JOCK & FREAK. And slap it on.

(Everyone changes place on stage.)

PERFECT. Wait!

(Everyone stops, annoyed. PERFECT finishes dressing, moves downstage, zips the fly on her skirt, then…)

PERFECT *(wondering why everyone is annoyed)*. What?
ALL. Gotta eat a…
JOCK. big breakfast…
PREP. quick breakfast…
PERFECT. skip breakfast…
AP *(overlapping with "breakfast")*. breakfast on the go.
FAITH *(simultaneous with "go")*. Going…
AP. Gone.

ALL. Homework?
FAITH, PREP, PERFECT. Some.
ALL. Homework?
AP & FREAK. Done.
ALL. Homework?
LONER. None.
ALL. Go, go, go, go.
FAITH. vitamin…
AP. Claritin…
PREP. Ritalin…
JOCK. Creatin…
REBEL. Mescaline…
FREAK. Pop a pill…
PERFECT. Pop "the pill."

(A car horn honks.)

FAITH. My cell?
PREP. My stash?
REBEL. My Crosby, Stills and Nash.

(Actors ad lib, confused on who she is talking about, i.e., "What?", "Crosby who?"

Horn honks. Projected: a digital clock that reads 7:48.)

ALL. We're late.
FREAK, PREP, JOCK, PERFECT. …jump in the car…
LONER & AP. …wait for the bus…
FAITH. …off for a walk…
REBEL *(walk faster)*. …for a run…
ALL. What's up?

LONER. Hey.
REBEL. Yo.
JOCK. 'Sup?
PREP. Yeah?
PERFECT. No?
FAITH. So…
AP. Way.
FREAK. Yeah.
PREP. I heard…
PERFECT. He is?
FAITH. To who?
PERFECT. To you?
REBEL. And him.
PERFECT. I know.
LONER. Whoa
FREAK. No
REBEL. So
AP. Hi
PERFECT. Whore
JOCK. Ho
ALL. Fuck.
AP. Time to go.
REBEL. One more smoke.
PERFECT. One more kiss.
JOCK. One more minute…
PREP. to take a piss.
FAITH. A pee.
AP. A poo. *(Beat.)* Oh, God I hate crapping in the school
    bathroom.
ALL. I'll meet you in the…
LONER. Hallway or…
FREAK. Homeroom or…

AP. Study or...
FAITH. Store or the...

   (ALL speak phrases in parenthesis.)

PERFECT. (The Caf) or the lab or the gym (by the door)
REBEL. By the north side of commons (the corner)
PREP. The gate so let's (wait)
JOCK. (Wait in the spot) in the back parking lot where it's
    (paved) and I'm
ALL (saved). by the...

   *(School bell rings. The actors dash offstage, as if they
   were late for class. Music: "Mad World" by Gary Jules[1]
   begins to play.)*

SELECTION

   *(Six props descend from above: a white baseball cap, a
   make-up compact, a pair of eyeglasses, a pack of cigarettes, a beaded leather choker and a cross necklace.*

   *LONER enters, examining his new surroundings, and the
   choices he can make. He wanders a bit farther downstage.*

   *LONER hides as FREAK enters. He watches FREAK
   wander among the various props dangling above his
   head. FREAK examines the baseball cap. PERFECT,
   REBEL and FAITH cross down, ignoring FREAK.
   FREAK crosses to the edge of the stage and sits.*

1 See copyright page for note on suggested music.

LONER, unnoticed by the others, sits to the side and watches the following.

FAITH crosses down and joins PERFECT and REBEL who are standing around the make-up compact. After a moment, they all three go for the compact, but PERFECT grabs it first. REBEL wanders away. FAITH follows. REBEL picks up the cigarettes and gestures to let FAITH have one. FAITH, a bit uneasy, moves away and grabs the cross necklace, blesses herself. REBEL, indifferent, pulls out a cigarette.

AP and JOCK cross into the light. AP immediately approaches the white baseball cap, and jumps, but it is out of his reach. Seeing AP's struggle, JOCK approaches and swiftly grabs the baseball cap on his first try. PERFECT is impressed.

PREP crosses down, determined. He walks around and observes, while waiting for the right moment to choose the most coveted prop. He picks up the glasses as AP picks up the choker. Unhappy with his choice, PREP crosses to AP and grabs the choker; AP is taken aback. As an afterthought, PREP hands the glasses to AP.

In unison AP, PREP, PERFECT, REBEL, FAITH and JOCK use their props to assume their identities. FREAK and LONER, not sure of where they should be, wander among the students. FREAK and LONER find each other. There are no props left.)

FREAK *(breaking the ice)*. Hey.
LONER *(timid response)*. Hey.

IDENTITY

(The characters are unaware of one another during this section, with the exception of unison text. Bell rings. Light goes to PERFECT.)

FAITH. She's nice.
AP. Ton of friends, knows everyone.
JOCK. She's cool.
REBEL. She hangs with jocks.
PREP. Drinks…like a horse.
FAITH. One can assume she drinks.
PREP. We all party together.
FREAK. She's a bitch.
LONER. We don't hang out but she's okay.

(Lights on JOCK.)

REBEL. A jock.
FAITH. Hardworking. Very determined.
AP. Yeah, he's a jock but he's different from what you would think.
PERFECT. He's really cool, very friendly with everyone. Sweet.
PREP. One of my best friends.
FREAK. Shining star of our school. Shining.
LONER. We spoke once in the sixth grade.

(Lights on AP.)

JOCK. Smart.
PERFECT. Very smart.

LONER. Helluva Doom player.
FAITH. Really nice kid.
REBEL. Loser.
FREAK. A little obsessed with school.
PREP. Don't know much about him.

(Lights to REBEL.)

LONER. She's cool.
PERFECT. She's crazy.
JOCK. She's okay. She's just...
AP. Different. Weird, but cool weird.
FREAK. I think she has a nipple pierced.
PERFECT. Tries to make a statement. I'd bet she's a really
    nice person inside.
PREP. Her older sister's cool.

(Lights on FREAK.)

FAITH. Smart.
JOCK. Computer...dude.
REBEL. Intense.
PERFECT. Insane.
PREP. We don't hang out. I don't know if he hangs out.
LONER. Crazy, anal, fucked-up sense of humor...and a
    good friend.

(Lights to PREP.)

JOCK. Oh, him...a dork.
PERFECT. So funny.
FAITH. Knows everyone.

AP. Party guy.

FREAK. Complete asshole.

PERFECT. People have the wrong idea about him. He's really sweet.

REBEL. I don't dare comment.

LONER. He has his head completely stuck up his ass.

(Lights to FAITH.)

PERFECT. Nice.

AP. Nice.

REBEL. She's nice.

JOCK. Smart. You know…

FREAK. I sit next to her in chemistry.

LONER. Dull. Boring and dull.

PREP. Needs to loosen up.

(Lights on LONER.)

PERFECT. I don't know him.

AP. Sits with us at lunch.

REBEL. Goofy…

ALL. Huh?

REBEL. …like the dog.

ALL. Oh.

FAITH. Definitely keeps to himself.

JOCK. Yeah…who?

PREP. No. Really can't say.

FREAK. A bit of a pussy, but a great friend. Yeah…

(Lights on AP.)

AP. People say I do well in school. I get along with everyone. You know, pretty average.

(AP exits. Lights on PREP.)

PREP. People say I'm cool. Likes to party. Friends with
everyone. Average guy.

(PREP exits. Lights on PERFECT.)

PERFECT. People say I'm nice. Friendly. Social. Make
people feel welcome. I don't know…

(PERFECT exits. Lights on REBEL.)

REBEL. People say I'm different. Goth even. Maybe even
druggie. Yeah, I get a lot of that.

(REBEL exits. Lights on FREAK.)

FREAK. I don't know what people say. Smart, funny.

(FREAK exits. Lights on JOCK.)

JOCK. People say I'm a jock, I'm sure. But I really hate
that. When people get to know me, they forget about
that.

(JOCK exits. Lights on FAITH.)

FAITH. People say I'm nice. Friendly…I don't know. Like
everyone else?

(FAITH exits. Lights on LONER.)

LONER. umm…I don't know.

GUIDANCE: PART I

VOICE (Prep). Okay, we'll start with the big question: what do you want to do with the rest of your life?

LONER. Hum?

VOICE. What are your interests?

LONER. I dunno.

VOICE. You don't know? *(Throwing an idea out there.)* You've run sound for the drama program. You clearly have a creative side.

LONER. Ah…I don't know.

VOICE *(pulling a compliment from the file)*. Nice work on the Frankenstein play. It was great, and the sounds when the monster came to life were incredible. I imagine the equipment must be complicated.

LONER *(dryly)*. It was a tape deck. I pushed play.

VOICE. Well, I know you're good with electronics, wise guy. I've seen you in the computer lab after school a bunch of times.

LONER. Yeah… *(He laughs.)*

VOICE. What?

LONER. Nothing.

VOICE *(back on track)*. Thought about getting a job in computers?

LONER. I don't know. It's kinda difficult to find a technician job when I'm only sixteen years old. *(Seeing if he's paying attention.)* It's a tough market for inexperienced, untrained hackers.

VOICE. Right, well there's lots of money to be made there.

LONER. Yeah. *(He laughs.)*

VOICE. What?

LONER. Nothing.

VOICE. You're not keeping secrets, are you?

LONER. Well, actually…

VOICE. C'mon, you can tell me…

LONER. Okay…

(Lights and sound change, showing we are in LONER's mind. He shifts his position to get a better look.)

LONER. …you have something hanging out of your nose.

VOICE. That's okay. You don't have to tell me.

LONER. Can't you feel that? It's a very large piece of snot.

VOICE. Well, you have a very creative mind.

LONER. It's like clinging to your nose hair.

VOICE. And I see you are taking Creative Writing?

LONER. Will you please wipe it off?

VOICE. Have you thought about majoring in Creative Writing?

LONER. I don't have a fucking clue what I'll major in, asshole. I'm dealing with the immediate here, and that should be okay. Why do we always have to know where we are going? And who's supposed to be guiding us? You? That's fucking hysterical. How are you qualified to guide me when you don't know the first thing about me? Yes, with a subtle glance from my file you glean that D in Political Science, or if you really want to impress the name of the show I did sound on. But let's see you name a friend, or the music I like…or where will I eat lunch today…and why do I eat lunch there? *(Notices something.)* Oh, shit…there's the twitch. Uh-oh, Mr. Booger, he's on to you. Ah, well. Go on… *(Beat, angrily.)* Go on. Just wipe it away. You can't just ignore it. *(Beat.)* Maybe you can. It avoids the embarrassment, the awkward situation. Lucky for you, Little Buddy, he's gonna pretend that you don't exist. Too bad we don't have that in common.

(Bell rings.)

CAFETERIA

(FAITH enters, leading a tour.)

FAITH *(to the audience).* Okay, is everybody here? Is everybody listening? Come on, I need to know if you are with me. *(Makes the audience respond.)* Super awesome! Now…we are about to enter the cafeteria. In eighth grade you probably have closed lunches, but here you can leave if you want. It's a bit crowded in here today 'cause of the rain. A lot of these people usually eat outside. *(LONER enters with a tray; looking for a place to sit.)* So let's see…where that kid is coming out *(points to LONER carrying the tray)* that's where they serve the lunches. *(LONER moves to get out of the way.)* Oh, and over that archway is our school motto…

(Projected: "Through these halls pass the finest kids in America.")

Through these halls pass the finest kids in America.

AP *(seated at one of the tables).* Which is not supposed to be ironic.

FAITH. Okay, vending machines are over here... *(LONER moves to get out of her way, look for a place to sit.)* Well, you pretty much can sit where you like. There are no assigned seats by grade or group. *(Secretly with the audience.)* Mostly, freshmen over there. Over there are the guys who wear their ball caps sideways known as the gangstas...not to be confused with the minorities. *(Realizing what she has said.)* I mean, some of them are, but... *(Getting flush.)* My point is, people sit with other people like them. How do I describe it?

REBEL. Segregation?

FAITH. Yes. *(Thinks about this, then...)* No... *(LONER returns to the space.)* Hey, *(pointing out an empty seat)* there's a spot over here.

(She points to a table with PREP and PERFECT. Not wanting to make a scene, LONER sits.)

LONER. Thanks.

FAITH. Anyway...here are the new restrooms. They're pretty awesome. They actually have sinks that you don't have to turn on the water, you just... *(Indicates putting hands under the faucet, making a water noise.)* I'm gonna make a quick stop and I'll be right back.

(FAITH crosses downstage, as lights change to the restroom. PERFECT applies make-up, studying herself in the mirror. REBEL smokes a cigarette off in the corner.)

FAITH. Hey. *(PERFECT looks at FAITH, then returns to applying her make-up.)* You won't believe what happened. I just added a new part to the tour, completely off the cuff. It was crazy.

PERFECT. You know, you would be really pretty if you straightened your hair.

FAITH. Thanks. I like your shirt.

PERFECT. I like yours too. Did you make it?

FAITH. No, I just… *(realizing the insult)* oh, no.

(PERFECT laughs. REBEL approaches.)

REBEL *(referring to PERFECT's shirt)*. Do you think cigarette burns would compeiment that color?

PERFECT. Fucking dyke. *(PERFECT exits.)*

FAITH. Thanks—

(REBEL ignores her and walks away. FAITH takes a beat, then walks to the audience. Lights change, we're out of the bathroom.)

FAITH *(regaining her composure)*. Okay. Next stop, the heart and soul of school: our gym. *(FAITH exits.)*

PREP. I think that seat's kinda taken.

LONER. I couldn't find another one.

PREP. Okay, that's cool. *(Beat.)* I've never really seen you before.

LONER. Ha, ha.

PREP. How long have you gone here? *(LONER doesn't say anything; just eats.)* No, seriously.

LONER. Come on, lay off.

PREP. I'm being serious. Did you transfer in?

LONER. Just let me eat. Okay? It's fuckin' pouring out.

PREP *(unseen to LONER, he signals to JOCK across the room)*. Okay, just trying to start a friendly conversation. Sorry, man. *(JOCK tosses a ketchup packet that hits LONER; to JOCK.)* What the fuck, asshole? Chill out, man. You hit me. *(JOCK laughs; LONER looks carefully at PREP; to LONER.)* He can be a real dickhead.

LONER. Yeah. *(Appreciating the kindness.)* Thanks. *(PREP signals again, as LONER takes a bite of food. Another packet hits LONER. This time both PREP and JOCK laugh. To PREP.)* There's much easier ways of impressing him, faggot.

(JOCK pulls out the seat as LONER gets up causing him to fall, dropping his tray and food. The cafeteria bursts out in laughter then freezes.)

PREP. You asked for that, faggot. You act like I disgust you? Fuck you, you disgust me. The greasy hair, this combat grunge, all of this. If this is truly who you are, then good for you. Congratulations on being yourself. *(Beat.)* I'm sorry your life sucks, but you chose this, right? You wanted to be you, and I want to be... *(Looks at JOCK, then back to LONER.)* You know, someday you'll remember high school as the sick feeling you got every day around noon trying to find a place to eat lunch and I'll remember it as the best years of my life...even if it's not me, the real me. *(Leans into LONER.)* Oh, which me am I talking about? Who is the real me? *(PREP looks around the group. He kisses JOCK.)* No one. He doesn't exist.

(Unfreeze.)

JOCK. I think you're in my seat.

(Bell rings. All leave as LONER picks up his food. RE-BEL approaches.)

REBEL. Sticks and stones…come on. *(REBEL moves closer to him.)* What's in a name? *(LONER abruptly stands, and starts to go.)* Hey, you dropped this. *(She throws a copy of* Romeo and Juliet *at him. He picks it up.)* I could use some help next period going over my lines…if you're free. *(REBEL exits. LONER reads poorly.)*

DRAMA

LONER. But soft! What light through yonder window breaks?
     It is the East, and Juliet is the sun!
     It is my lady; O, it is my love!
     Juliet enters from above.
REBEL. Um…just the lines.
LONER. Oh, yeah. Right. *(REBEL puts on a rehearsal skirt.)*
     It is my lady; O, it is my love!
(He looks at REBEL, and she freezes. He reads with genuine feeling.)
     O that she knew she were!
     She speaks, yet she says nothing. What of that?
     Her eye discourses; I will answer it.
     I am too bold; 'tis not to me she speaks.

(LONER freezes, as REBEL unfreezes.)

REBEL. Yeah, well, it's probably this play, and that thing that happens when you're on stage, not being your-self...but I look at you, and let's face it, you're not my first choice—maybe not anyone's: the long baby face, with the Jay Leno chin, and—but when I look at me...I see someone too familiar staring back at me. I see the overpriced life she lives in. I see all that spelled out in every fat bulge, or frizz, or nose that's uncoverable... I'm uncomfortable with me. So I look away...to some-thing else, someone else and you're not so bad...you are possible, obtainable. If I don't look at you and see that, then there's not much left, but some weed, and another episode of *Friends*, and my pathetic antisocial fucked-up life. So hey, it's your chance...climb the balcony... give me a plastic rose...and we'll pretend that we're ac-tually beautiful people. Come on, it's easy to escape.

(REBEL kneels on two chairs which function as the bal-cony. LONER unfreezes, and looks to her.)

REBEL. O Romeo, Romeo! wherefore art thou Romeo?
    Deny thy father and refuse thy name!
    Or, if thou wilt not, be but sworn my love,
    And I'll no longer be a Capulet.
LONER *(crossing to her, addressing her)*. Shall I hear more, or shall I speak at this?

(Awkward pause. The bell rings. JOCK, AP, PREP, FAITH and PERFECT enter, and voice the thoughts in LONER's head. During this session, REBEL packs props

in her backpack, runs lines, going over blocking, occa-
sionally glancing at LONER. She is going through her
own decision-making process.)

LONER *(staring at REBEL)*. All I need is a...
ACTOR (Prep). Word.
ACTOR (Perfect). A simple word.
ACTOR (AP). It would open up a tremendous
ALL. Conversation.
ACTOR (Jock). Just turn to her
ACTOR (Perfect). And look at her
ACTOR (AP). Open your mouth
ACTOR (Prep). And say...
ACTOR (Faith). Sorry this sounds so awkward. I think you
    act really good.
ACTOR (Jock) *(commenting on the previous)*. "Act really
    good"?
ACTOR (AP). And sound really awkward so
ACTOR (Prep). No. Never.
ACTOR (Perfect). Can't take the rejection
ACTOR (Faith). Can't take the humiliation if
ACTOR (Jock). Someone else found out.
ACTOR (Perfect). She would talk.
ACTOR (Prep). She would say my name. She would...
ACTOR (Faith) *(imagining her speaking his name)*. Say
    my name?
ACTOR (AP). ...actually coming from her lips.
ACTOR (Perfect). Oh God, tongue in mouth.
ACTOR (AP). Touching her nipples with my tongue. Nip-
    ping small bites
ACTOR (Jock). My fingers

ACTOR (Faith). Rubbing across her breast. She would like it.

ACTOR (Prep). She would want it.

ACTOR (Perfect). Here. On the desk.

ALL *(visualizing it)*. Yeah.

ACTOR (Faith). Think of the sex. Feeling it after I was finished. A space in her juicy—

ALL *(looking away)*. Oh God.

(LONER deals with his erection.)

ACTOR (Prep). Stop it. Get down.

(REBEL tosses a pencil in LONER's direction.)

ALL *(freezing)*. Shit.

ACTOR (AP). She can see me sweat.

ALL. Shhh!

ACTOR (AP). She knows I am acting crazy.

ALL. Shhh!

(REBEL, annoyed, picks it up herself.)

ACTOR (Perfect). Okay. That's it.

ACTOR (Prep). I gotta go.

(LONER goes to leave.)

ALL. Wait…

ACTOR (Faith). Maybe if I

ACTOR (AP). Say that I

ACTOR (Perfect). Wonder if you

ACTOR (Prep). Now while I'm walking by.

ALL. Casually

ACTOR (Faith). Seize it. Talk to her. It's not even talk. It's a...

ALL. Hi.

ACTOR (Jock). "Hi" is gay. That's all I need is to sound like a fag.

ACTOR (Prep). But if I just say something.

ACTOR (AP). Saying one thing could change everything.

ACTOR (Jock). Go ahead.

ACTOR (Prep). Come on!

ALL. WHAT ARE YOU WAITING FOR?

(Bell rings. REBEL exits. LONER looks away. Lighting changes as students change the space into a classroom.)

ACTOR (Perfect). And what would we talk about? Nothing. Not a fucking thing. What would a snotty little cunt like her say to a piece of shit like me?

ACTOR (AP). What was I thinking?

ACTOR (Prep). She's a bitch.

ACTOR (Faith). Bitch.

ACTOR (Perfect). And I am not stupid enough to fall into her trap.

ACTOR (Jock). Let her tell the whole school what the freak did.

ACTOR (AP). One thing after another...

ACTOR (Faith). Leading to more

ACTOR (Prep). And more...

ACTOR (Perfect). No way. No fucking way.

(REBEL returns and sits next to him. The space is now a classroom.)

REBEL. Do you have the time?

LONER. No. *(REBEL looks away.)* But thanks for the play...today.

REBEL. What?

LONER. I liked the play.

REBEL. Thanks, but I didn't write it.

LONER. Yeah, but it was a good play... *(They laugh.)* It's 1:15...6th period.

REBEL. Yeah, I know. *(Awkward but they smile.)* Hey, I'm...

(JOCK sits right next to LONER.)

JOCK. I thought you were gay. *(REBEL exits. LONER turns to JOCK.)* What?

CREATIVE WRITING

(REBEL's voice amplified from offstage throughout this scene.)

TEACHER. Okay, let's critique the last of the narrative assignments. I'll follow along with your essay and share my comments. You're up.

(LONER stands in front of the class. His essay is projected. The TEACHER's corrections appear as she critiques his essay.)

LONER *(uncertain, in a low voice)*. The town, even at 1:00 a.m., was still…

PERFECT. I can't hear what he's saying.

FAITH. Shhhh.

(PERFECT shushes FAITH.)

TEACHER. You need to speak a little louder.

LONER *(a bit more confident)*. The town, even at 1:00 a.m., was still bustling with activity as the man dressed in black walked down the empty streets.

TEACHER. Great opening.

LONER. The moon was barely visible, hiding under a shield of clouds, adding a chill…

TEACHER. …which added a chill…

LONER. …which added a chill to the atmosphere. What was most recognized about the man was the jingling of his belt chains striking not only the two visible guns, but the large Bowie knife, slung in anticipation of use.

TEACHER. Great details. Well done.

(A laugh from PREP and JOCK. LONER stares at them, as the lights shift and sounds occur. We are now in LONER's mind. A light comes up which projects a large shadow on the chalk slate. LONER walks into the light, glaring at the students.)

LONER. In the midst of the nightlife in the center of the average-sized town, this man walked, fueled by some untold purpose, what Christians would call evil.

TEACHER. New paragraph.

LONER *(turns and looks at the shadow)*. His face was entirely in shadow, yet I could feel his anger, cutting through the air like a razor. He noticed my presence but paid no attention as he kept walking toward a popular bar. The Watering Hole. He stopped and waited. "For whom?" I wondered, as I saw them step out. A group of college-preps...the second-largest spoke up:

(The students in the class become the college-preps in the story.)

LONER & PREP. Nice trench coat, dude. That's pretty cool.

LONER. The man in black said nothing but I could feel his anger growing.

LONER & PREP. "You want a fight? C'mon, put the guns away, fuckin' pussy!!!"

TEACHER. Please...

LONER. Other preps could be heard muttering in the background...

LONER & AP. "C'mon, man, you wouldn't shoot us. We're in the middle of a public place."

LONER. Yet the comment I remember the most was uttered from the biggest of the group, obviously a cocky, power-hungry prick.

TEACHER. I thought I said...

LONER & JOCK. "Go ahead, man! Shoot me!!! I want you to shoot me!!! Ha, ha. You won't. Goddamn pussy..."

TEACHER. And I've stopped commenting—

LONER. It was faint at first but grew in intensity and power as I heard the man laugh. *(Kids start laughing; under their laugh...)* For almost half a minute this laugh, spawned from the most powerful place conceivable, filled the air, and through the entire town, the entire world...

(As the laugh gets unbearably intense, LONER pulls out an imaginary shotgun and fires on the students. Real gunshots are heard. All of the students fall to the ground, dead. The TEACHER's voice remains unaffected.)

TEACHER. New paragraph.

LONER. The town was utterly still. He stopped, and gave me a look I will never forget. If I could face an emotion of God, it would have looked like the man. I not only saw in his face, but also felt emanating from him, power, complacence, closure and godliness. The man smiled, and in that instant, I understood his actions.

TEACHER. Okay. *(Class unfreezes, lights shift back to normal. LONER walks to his seat.)* Stay up there. Now, before I accept this draft, cut out all the inappropriate language. But, the profanity notwithstanding, let's open it up for discussion. Comments? *(To AP.)* Yes.

AP. I thought it was unique.

TEACHER. What do you mean by that?

AP. He has a very distinct voice, and was careful about the details.

JOCK. Come on.

TEACHER. Yes? What do you think?

JOCK *(long awkward pause)*. I don't know...I didn't like it.

TEACHER. Why?

JOCK. Are you serious? What do you want me to say? It sucks.

(PREP laughs.)

TEACHER. All right. Some courtesy please.

JOCK. Look, call on someone else. I'll tell him what I think later on.

LONER. Tell me now. I'm right here.

TEACHER. That's enough!

JOCK. I mean, what if I wrote a little story about cleaning up the school, taking out people like him?

TEACHER. One more outburst like that, and you are out of here!

(JOCK stands, the class freezes, and lights shift.)

JOCK. What? You're going to kick me out? Are you serious? This piece of shit writes about walking around the town shooting people for no reason, and you want me to what…to give constructive criticism? How about "throw this maniac out, and get him some fucking help"? Was I supposed to feel sorry for him or something? Look at him. What has he done to earn anyone's respect? What time did he wake up this morning? Seven? Seven-thirty? Try five a.m. I ran four miles before he even got out of bed this morning. And while he's home after school circle jerking to Laura Croft with his faggot-ass friends, I'll still be here, serving the school you teach in. Whether I feel like it or not, I'll show up and work. What does he do? Nothing. So, that's what he is: nobody. And, you know what, Teach? I'm valuable, and you should show me the respect I deserve.

(The bell rings. Lights shift back. JOCK hesitates, waiting for LONER as the rest of the class gets up to go.)

TEACHER. We're going to talk about this at the beginning of class tomorrow. Do you understand?

JOCK. Yeah. I understand.

TEACHER *(to LONER)*. Stay here for a second. *(LONER crosses downstage, and JOCK glares at him as he slowly exits the stage.)* Can you come by my office after school? I'd like to talk to you about your story before I give you a grade.

LONER. Why?

TEACHER. You are an excellent writer, but I have some problems with this one.

(Students at lockers, in the hall. LONER leaves with new confidence as he passes FREAK.)

LONER. Hey.

FREAK. Hey.

(JOCK shoulders LONER to the ground. PERFECT and PREP notice. All freeze. FREAK helps LONER up. Projected on the slate are the English translations.)

FREAK. Srichst du deustch? *(Do you speak German?)*

(To JOCK as he walks by.)

LONER. Er ist ein Arschloch. *(He's a fucking asshole.)* How's that?

(To PERFECT.)

FREAK. Not as good as... Sie ist eine Schlampe. *(She's a sloppy whore.)*
LONER. Well, how about...

(To PREP.)

LONER & FREAK. Ich will dich toten! *(I want to kill you!)*

(They laugh at the coincidence. Bell rings. All unfreeze.)

LONER. Later.
FREAK. Later.

(All exit as FREAK sits.)

GUIDANCE: PART II

VOICE (Jock). So what are your interests? *(Beat.)* You must have something. Looks here like you played soccer, is that right?
FREAK. Yeah.
VOICE. What did you enjoy about soccer?
FREAK. I don't know.
VOICE. Come on, tell me more then "I don't know..." You're a bright kid. Your grades are excellent. What about the future? Any post-graduate plans? *(FREAK goes to talk; he interrupts.)* Come on...
FREAK. Marines or computer science maybe.

VOICE. Marines, huh? That's great. You know, even the Marines would like to see an extra-curricular activity on your transcript.

FREAK. Well then you should write one in there and help me out. *(FREAK laughs. Counselor does not.)*

VOICE. Your transcript shows you've been to a bunch of different schools in the past few years. *(Beat.)*

FREAK. Uh-huh.

VOICE. Why is that?

FREAK. Because I've been to a bunch of different schools in the past few years.

VOICE. You've moved around a lot?

FREAK. Yup.

VOICE. That couldn't have been easy.

FREAK. Is that a question or a statement?

VOICE. What?

FREAK. My dad's in the military, so we went where the work was.

VOICE. That explains the interest in the Marines, huh? Yeah, well, good. Good. But like I said, even the Marines would like to see an extra-curricular activity. Shows commitment, discipline. Picking up a sport could take care of all that.

(Sound and lights shift. FREAK begins to speak his thoughts. The counselor takes no notice.)

FREAK. Would it take care of the fact that I get pissed off so easily? That I freak out at almost anything?

VOICE. Two years on a sport can fix up your Marine application.

FREAK. How do you fix up the fact that I'm pigeon-
  chested, or that my dosage has been increased?
VOICE. I don't know why someone as bright as you isn't
  involved in more activities?
FREAK. I don't know why you keep glancing at my shirt.
VOICE. Do any of your friends play soccer?
FREAK. FRIEND, but thanks for asking, you little fucked-
  up man, with your bachelor's degree in business on your
  wall next to the three-day certificate in counseling. You
  are not equipped to handle what's going on inside of me.
  You want me to open up to you in one conversation? I
  don't think I'll be telling you anything today, sir, because I've just been humiliated. But I'll let you in on a
  little secret... *(leans in)* I'm looking at a man, who is
  disgusted by me, sir, by the way I dress, by my choice
  of silence. He's looking right at me and actually thinks
  that I can't see right through him. But see, sir, I actually
  can see the sports page opened under my file. But see,
  he thinks I can't see that. I wonder why he would think
  that? *(Beat.)* No. No. I've decided that in our little ten-
  minute session I don't think we're going to be friends...
  because I'm smarter than you are, and I have something
  you don't have: self-awareness. You want to help me
  figure out the next eighty years of my life, why don't we
  start with today, or what's going to happen when the
  bell rings ten minutes from now? Tell me why I have a
  short temper and get angry at almost anything I don't
  like, like people I have no respect for trying to tell me
  what to do. Or why I have too many inside jokes or
  thoughts to have very many friends. You tell me why.
  And then we can talk. Okay? *(FREAK reaches back and
  swings wildly at the invisible wall and punches it. Sharp*

sounds of a wall shattering, glass breaking. Lights and sound change.)

VOICE. Well, I'll see you in a few months.

FREAK. Okay. Sorry I was so silent. Lots to think about.

VOICE. No problem. And hey, I hope you'll think about what I suggested. It really would be great for you.

FREAK. And what was that, again?

VOICE. Catch…

PHYSICAL EDUCATION

(A basketball is thrown at FREAK from above. Whistle blows. A scoreboard is projected on the screen, onto which the two teams, Shirts and Skins, are indicated. PREP, AP and JOCK enter. AP and JOCK are shirtless and move to one side. PREP and FREAK are on the other. JOCK takes the ball from FREAK.)

JOCK. Okay, 8 all. Let's go.

PREP. No, we're out of time.

JOCK. Come on. *(To AP.)* Let's go.

(PREP shoves the ball into AP's stomach. AP turns to JOCK, anxious and confused.)

AP. Start from anywhere, or…?

FREAK. Throw it from out-of-bounds!

(FREAK and PREP laugh. JOCK sees AP is nervous.)

JOCK. Time out. *(He pulls AP aside, puts his arm around him.)*

FREAK. Time out? We have like two minutes. *(JOCK glares at him; FREAK gets pissed.)*

JOCK *(aside, to AP)*. All right, dude, here's what we're gonna do, I'm gonna throw it in bounds to you, they're both gonna try and attack you...

AP. I've picked up on that pattern, yeah...

JOCK *(drawing on his hand)*. All you have to do is pivot and bounce pass, okay? That's it. Pivot and pass. *(JOCK takes the ball, goes out of bounds to throw the ball into the court.)*

AP. Is pivot, is it what it sounds like, I mean, do you want me to—*(tries to pivot)*?

(FREAK and PREP laugh.)

JOCK. Dude, yes. Just... *(He pivots, his back to FREAK and PREP, mimes passing.)*

PREP. C'mon...

(They set up for the play. Whistle blows. JOCK tosses the ball to AP and performs a quick move to get away from PREP. He motions to AP.)

JOCK. Now! Now!

(FREAK has already glued himself to AP; after a brief "jump ball," he shoves AP, who falls to the ground.)

PREP. Jump ball.
JOCK. Fuck you, jump ball. Foul. He shoved him!
PREP. Whatever.
AP. I'm sorry...

JOCK *(to AP)*. Forget it. You get two free throws. A point a piece. We just need one to win. *(AP crosses to the opposite foul line. PREP and FREAK laugh.)* Over here. *(AP crosses to the Shirts' side of the stage, and take his place. FREAK, PREP and JOCK flank him.)* Focus. You gotta see it in your head.

(AP focuses on the shot, takes a big breath, and flings it offstage. Buzzer sounds.)

AP. Shit.

JOCK. You've got another shot.

AP. Oh good.

JOCK. Focus, breathe, see the shot, and shoot.

AP. Focus, breathe, see the shot, and shoot. *(AP focuses on the shot, takes a big breath, and preps the ball; he hesitates.)* I can do this. Focus, breathe, see the shot, and shoot. *(AP focuses on the shot, takes a big breath, and preps the ball; he hesitates.)* I see it. But I see much more than the shot: *(looks at JOCK)* I see this guy who I shared Oreos and Power Rangers and the occasional Sonic the Hedgehog level with...look at me like a stranger because I can't get a stupid ball into a stupid hoop. So, what do I do? What can I do? Nothing, so just toss the ball and hope that they'll grow up and realize that all this will mean nothing. Great, I sound like my dad. "It's just a phase and when school is over everything will change." Makes sense, but how the fuck is that helpful to me NOW...with these people—yes, stupid people—who won't go away. *(He lifts the ball to shoot, trembling.)* Focus. Definite 4.2. Breathe. Information technology with a minor in artificial intelligence.

See the shot. I see all that so far away from me. Shoot...
(He tosses it offstage. Buzzer sounds. He got it in.)
JOCK. Awesome shot, man.
PREP. 9-8. Come on.
FREAK. Let's go.

(AP moves to the sidelines, while the others take their positions. Bell rings.)

JOCK. Oh well. Game.
FREAK. Fuck.
JOCK. Good game.
FREAK. FUCK!!!
JOCK. Chill out, man. Good game.

(JOCK offers his hand. FREAK exits. AP is now sitting on the gym floor, holding his knees to his chest.)

JOCK. What a freak, man. *(To PREP.)* Let's go.
PREP *(pointing to AP)*. Holy shit, he pissed himself!
JOCK. What?
PREP. Oh God...
JOCK. Pathetic.

(Bell rings. AP buries his head in his knees, as the kids laugh/mumble comments as they leave. We hear the sounds of AP fighting back tears as the lights shift to FREAK on a bench, changing out of his gym clothes. FREAK hesitates, waiting for the right moment to take off his shirt unseen. PREP and JOCK notice.)

PREP. Why does it take you so long to get undressed?

JOCK. He doesn't want us to see his tits.

PREP. Is that it? Is that why you never shower after class?

JOCK. No, he just doesn't shower.

FREAK. What's your problem, asshole?

JOCK. What'd you say?

FREAK. Nothing.

PREP. No, I think he called you an asshole.

FREAK *(with attitude)*. Okay…

> *(JOCK goes for FREAK and his shirt gets pulled off in the struggle. PREP and JOCK stare at his chest.)*

FREAK. Get off me.

PREP. Oh, shit! Look at his chest.

JOCK. Man…that's fucked up.

PREP. Are you missing something in there?

FREAK *(rising to get his shirt)*. I don't think so, dude.

JOCK *(keeping the shirt from FREAK)*. What do you call this sick shit?

FREAK. A chest deformity. What's *your* problem?

JOCK. Oh, you're so cool. You're my idol.

FREAK. What did I do to you, asshole?

JOCK *(drops the shirt, grabs FREAK's nipple and squeezes it slowly)*. Watch your mouth, you little bitch.

FREAK *(helplessly)*. Get off.

PREP *(tossing FREAK's shirt)*. Let him get dressed. He's making me sick. *(A pill bottle falls out of FREAK's shirt pocket. PREP picks up bottle.)* Pharmaceuticals…

JOCK. What is it? Viagra?

PREP. L-U-V-O-X

JOCK. Let me see it.

(AP enters.)

AP. Guys, the coach is rounding up... *(Sees the harassment.)* I—
PREP. Uh-oh, Freak, your girlfriend's here.
AP. The coach sent me in here to...
JOCK. Hey, what do you make of this shit? Huh?
AP. I don't know...um...
JOCK *(pronounced Love-vox)*. Luvox?
AP. Luvox... *(Pronounced Lou-vox.)* I think it's an anti-depressant.
JOCK. He's a mental case...
PREP. So, you're a faggot *and* you're depressed?
JOCK. Tell me seriously; do you like looking at my ass?

(JOCK wipes his ass with the pills which spill all over the stage. The voice of COACH is heard from offstage.)

COACH (Loner). Hey, what the hell's going on?
JOCK *(dropping the pill bottle, looking out above the audience)*. Hey, Coach.
COACH. What is this?

(Beat. PREP and JOCK look at each other.)

AP. We were just fooling around.
COACH. Well, get dressed and give me a hand outside. Boys...
JOCK *(to AP)*. Great shot, man.
AP. Thanks.

(Bell rings.

*FREAK glares at AP, as a classroom scene now sur-
rounds him. The students face the direction of the
TEACHER, whose voice resounds from the back of the
theater.)*

HISTORY LESSON

TEACHER (Faith). Who wants to tell me about Natural
    Selection? *(All groan.)* Survival of the fittest? Who did
    their reading last night? *(FREAK continues to pick up
    the pills. AP raises his hand.)* Yes?
AP. The theory of natural selection, or survival of the fit-
    test, has replaced creation stories like Adam and Eve in
    the Garden with a different, though equally questionable
    creation story we refer to as evolution.
TEACHER. Very good. Who would care to elaborate?
    Anyone? *(AP raises hand.)* Anyone else?

(Lights and sound indicate we are in FREAK's fantasy.)

FREAK *(an outburst)*. Survival of the fittest doesn't al-
    ways mean survival of the biggest. *(All "huh?" reac-
    tion.)* Sometimes…anything can make you the fittest in
    the right situation. *(All "oh" reaction.)*
TEACHER. Your theory could best be expressed through
    the Biblical story of Cain and Abel.
FREAK. My thought exactly.
TEACHER. Which is exactly why I had it.
AP. Which was the author's point.
FREAK. Shut the fuck up.

(Beat indicating "Did he say that?")

AP. Excuse me?

(FREAK points to TEACHER, "cuing" her.)

TEACHER. Sit down and shut the fuck up.
ALL. Yeah.

(AP sits down and shuts up.)

TEACHER. Shall I continue?
FREAK. Please do.
TEACHER. Abel, class, was the pretty boy, *(all react "Who?")* you know—the popular prep who sucked anyone's dick to get them to like him... *(all react "Oh")* while Cain was a bit more...
FREAK. ...misunderstood...
TEACHER. Exactly—and actually possessed some fucking brains... *(all laugh)* but in the end...Cain killed Abel. *(All "oooh.")* None of Abel's "fit" qualities helped him. In the end it was Cain who lived on...
FREAK. Presenting the man who Nature selected: Cain. The first murderer...
CAIN (Rebel). You're impressed.
FREAK. What did you use? A knife, a club, what?
CAIN. You want details?
FREAK. That's why you're here.
CAIN *(calling offstage)*. Abel... *(Back to FREAK.)*

(ABEL, played by AP, stands.)

ABEL. Yes?

FREAK. We're about to hear how you got your fuckin' head smashed in.

CAIN. I fuckin' smashed his head in. Shown here:

(Projected: A picture of CAIN holding ABEL's head up. All react. Projected: ABEL's spine still attached to his now-severed head. The group reacts, grossed out.)

ABEL. That's not in the Bible.

CAIN. Survival of the Fittest.

FREAK. You got the ball rolling...

CAIN. I got the fame. The most famous killing of all time.

(LEOPOLD and LOEB appear. PERFECT plays LEOPOLD. PREP is LOEB. Two distinguished gentlemen.)

LOEB. Pre-Noah's Ark, perhaps. But let's talk about the trial of the century...

CAIN. Who are these assholes?

(Projected are slides of the famous trial photos.)

TEACHER. On May 21, 1924, in Chicago, Nathan F. Leopold Jr., 19, and his friend Richard A. Loeb, 18, kidnapped 14-year-old Bobby Franks from his schoolyard and bludgeoned him to death. *(All "oooh.")* Their motive:

LEOPOLD & LOEB. Just for the hell of it.

TEACHER. Both of the young men were smart...

LEOPOLD. A genius. An IQ of 210.

LOEB. A graduate of the University of Michigan at 17.

FREAK. Of course. How else could they fuck with America?

TEACHER. Of good family background...

FREAK. Like me.

CAIN. Hey, why am I suddenly getting the backseat, here?

LOEB. Because we are examples of Nietzche's ubermen... *(introducing himself to FREAK)* ...Loeb.

FREAK. Ubermen?

LEOPOLD. ...better and smarter than normal humans. *(Introducing himself.)* ...Leopold.

LOEB *(suggesting CAIN)*. Because history is full of lone-wolf psychos...we were a team.

LEOPOLD. We were able to do together what we never would have done apart.

LOEB. Murder.

FREAK. Yeah?

LEOPOLD. The perfect murder.

CAIN. Except you were caught.

LOEB. As were you.

CAIN. I was caught by God. You idiots were nabbed by the police. This one dropped his glasses at the crime scene!

FREAK. What?

LEOPOLD. Details...

FREAK *(to CAIN)*. So I should work alone?

CAIN. No, you should choose your partner in crime wisely.

AP *(trying to get in on the action)*. Yeah.

ALL *(except AP)*. Shut up!

FREAK. Why did you do it? Go all the way. End someone's life.

LOEB. The perfect crime demands murder. It is a necessary element.

FREAK. How did you actually...I mean, actually follow through and...

LEOPOLD. And kill someone and stuff their body in a concrete drainage culvert?

FREAK *("not quite what I meant but...")*. Sure...

LOEB. You have to believe you are superior...that you are above the law and its consequences.

FREAK. Yeah, that's right.

TEACHER. Most interesting of all is the bizarre relationship of the two killers, who were widely regarded to have been...

LOEB *(attempting to interrupt)*. Brilliant...

LEOPOLD. Handsome.

TEACHER *(correcting them)*. Lovers.

(Long beat. FREAK stares at the two killers.)

CAIN. Oh, you are so busted.

AP. Yeah. *(They all turn their heads to say...)*. Shut up, I know. *(He sits.)*

FREAK. Fuckin' faggots. Kein mitleid!

ABEL. What does that mean?

(HITLER YOUTH, played by JOCK, appears.)

HITLER YOUTH. No mercy.

FREAK. Kill everything. Kill 'em all.

CAIN. Who the hell are you?

(The HITLER YOUTH salutes the "Heil Hitler." Projected are photos of the prototypical Hitler Youth.)

TEACHER. The Hitler Youth movement was a major force in rallying support around Hitler's vision of his own Aryan nation, his own attempt at Natural Selection...
FREAK *(saluting with the wrong hand)*. Heil Hit—
HITLER YOUTH *(stops him)*. The young man who only studies philosophy and in a time like this buries himself behind his books or sits at home by the fire, he is no German youth! I call upon you!

(The Hitler quotes are projected on the screen as the Youth speaks them, ending with: "—Adolph Hitler 1933.")

FREAK. What do I have to do? What do I have to learn?
HITLER YOUTH. Knowledge would spoil my young people. I prefer that they learn only what they pick up by following their own play instinct. But they must learn self-control.
FREAK. I'm in control... What else do I need?
HITLER YOUTH. IF A PEOPLE IS TO BECOME FREE IT NEEDS PRIDE AND WILL-POWER, DEFIANCE, *(+ LOEB)* HATE, *(+ LEOPOLD)* HATE, AND ONCE AGAIN *(+ CAIN)* HATE...
FREAK. You know what I...
ALL. Hate...
FREAK. I...
ALL. Hate...
FREAK. I...
HITLER YOUTH. And once again...

FREAK. ...*hate* when there is a group of assholes standing in the middle of a hallway or walkway, and they just stand there talking and blocking my fucking way!

HITLER YOUTH. Get the fuck outta the way or I'll bring a friggin' sawed-off shotgun to your house and blow your snotty-ass head off!

CAIN. You know what I hate?

FREAK. When people mispronounce words! And they don't even know it too. Like often, or acrosT, or eX-spreso, or pacific.

CAIN. I wanna get pacific witch-you.

FREAK. You know what I hate?

LEOPOLD. People who don't believe in personal hygiene.

ABEL. For the love of God, CLEAN UP!

FREAK. I hate everything unless I say otherwise, hey, don't follow your dreams or your goals or any of that shit, follow your fuckin' animal instincts. If it moves, kill it, if it doesn't, burn it. Kein mitleid!!!

(Industrial heavy metal music now sounds from back of the theater surrounding audience.)

ALL. KEIN MITLEID!

(Everyone stomps wildly to the music in the unison. The lyrics scroll on the screen:)

> *Du auf dem Schulhof*
> *ich zum Töten bereit*
> *und keiner hier weiss*
> *von meiner Einsamkeit*

(The group, consumed by violence, freezes. Lights switch immediately to the glow of a computer screen on FREAK's face, as he sits in front of a computer.)

FREAK. What does this mean?

(The lyrics appear on the screen as the group speaks them in unison.)

ALL. CHILDREN IN HALLWAYS
HAVE BLOOD ON THEIR HANDS
FOR NO ONE WOULD LEAVE ME ALONE

(On the screen we see a search engine projected. FREAK types the words "Bomb Building" into the entry box. The mouse moves toward the search engine. Projected is a black page with red lettering: "The Anarchist's Cookbook." The phone rings. Lights come up on PERFECT, an antsy customer waiting for her order.)

WORK

FREAK. Hello, Pizza Parlor. Please hold?
JOCK. Gimme a sausage, double cheese and—
FREAK *(to JOCK)*. Hang on… *(On the phone.)* Hello, Pizza Parlor. Please hold?

(More people wander in…)

PERFECT *(to JOCK)*. I was here first, sorry. Can I have half pepperoni and half mushroom?

FREAK. Yeah, hang on.

REBEL. Where's your bathroom?

FREAK. You can't use it. *(The phone rings.)* Hello?

MANAGER VOICE (AP). Hey, when you get a chance, I need a cheese and a pepperoni…

FREAK. Okay. *(On the phone.)* Hello, Pizza Parlor. Please hold?

PREP *(enters)*. I'm here for a pick-up. Three cheese pizzas— Helloooo?

(Everyone clamors for attention with ad libs, trying to get FREAK's attention. This overlaps with the MANAGER's voice becoming prominent as FREAK stares straight ahead, ignoring all of the commotion. The MANAGER's speech becomes a "countdown" for FREAK's cue to be "on TV.")

MANAGER VOICE. And…THREE extra cheese…TWO sausage…ONE pepperoni… You're on the air!

(All of the actors are silent and immediately plop down in front of FREAK, who is behind the counter of his "cooking show." Polite applause and cheesy intro music. On the screen is projected the live video feed focusing on FREAK, but occasionally showing the others as the "studio audience.")

FREAK. Hello and welcome. So…let's get started, shall we? You do not want to have the length any longer than eight inches. Diameter should usually be between three-quarter inch and two inches. Pipes are about as easy to purchase as a CD. The way I bought most of mine is by going out and getting all of the caps one day, then getting the pipes a few days later, or at a different store.

PERFECT. What if I want to save time and get the caps and pipes all at once?

FREAK. You can, but I wouldn't recommend it. You don't want to look too suspicious.

PERFECT. Thanks.

FREAK. You really don't have to spend a day making the perfect powder. If you're eighteen you can buy this shit at almost any store. Start pouring your—

PREP. Can I do this at home?

FREAK. Yes, but when in your bedroom be sure you have plenty of newspaper down because accidents do happen and if you have a big stain on your carpet, Mom and Dad might ask some questions. *(General ad libs, "I hate when that happens...", "that's my mom...", etc.)* The ingredients used are very important if you want to kill and injure a lot of people. From broken paperclips to two-inch nails to solder...

JOCK. Yes, what about buckshot? Will that work?

FREAK. Good question. Almost anything small and metal will work. Go ahead and start pouring your powder/ shrapnel shit in. After it's about half full, tap it on a hard surface until it will not settle anymore.

PREP. Do I have to tap?

FREAK. Absolutely. You want as much powder as physically possible in there. Once it is full, screw on the cap and you're basically ready to go.

(With the MANAGER's voice, the light changes. The actors return to the hustle of the pizza place as they exit.)

MANAGER VOICE. What the hell is that?

FREAK. Nothing.

MANAGER VOICE. Jesus Christ…

FREAK. It's not real.

MANAGER VOICE. Fireworks are one thing, but a god-damn pipe bomb?

FREAK. No problem. It's totally cool. Sorry.

(FAITH enters, almost getting run over by the others exiting, and stands back as if reading the menu above the counter. The phone rings.)

MANAGER VOICE. We'll deal with this later. Put it away and take her order.

(FREAK waits until he goes. He starts to pace and freak out.)

FREAK *(under his breath)*. FUCK. FUCK ME. FUCK.

(He turns around as FAITH comes up to the counter.)

FAITH. I'd like a veggie supreme. I think…

FREAK *(tense)*. One second, please.

FAITH. I'd like a *(looking down from menu)* …oh, hey. Hey. I didn't know you worked here. I'm—you know, from fifth period…

FREAK. Jesus Christ, fuck off. *(FREAK freezes.)*

FAITH. Okay…okay… *(At a loss, starts to tear up. Directs the following to God.)* I just don't understand. Jesus, tell me, is this normal? Is this healthy? Because they, they… love their lives. They are smiling, laughing, happy people. Those faces, those photos are on the cover of my *Teenage Spiritual Guide* from youth group. Those faces...not this face. Look at this face. Why isn't it on your book? *(Beat.)* I'm sorry but this feeling of being saved...this knowing that at least I will be saved...it's making me sick. If this is what You went through, I understand suffering. But why torture me? Because they tortured You? Then take me now. Take me right now. It seems death on a cross, a few hours of suffocation, is nothing next to four years of looks, and smirks and "fuck-off's." I don't know, Lord. You tell me. Maybe that's why Your teenage years are such a mystery. You didn't want anyone to know. *(Beat.)* Will You respond? I already know the answer to that, but I wonder...will I ever see Your face? What will it feel like looking in Your eyes...or any man's eyes? The reassurance of "It's all right" from a voice you can actually hear. Nothing imagined or blindly trusted. His kiss...what would he taste like...?

(FREAK unfreezes.)

FREAK. Hey...
FAITH. Oh God...gosh...
FREAK. Hey, I'm sorry. I'm really sorry.
FAITH. No, it's...I'm not feeling well.
FREAK. Do you want some Coke?
FAITH. Uh...no... *(Beat.)*
FREAK. Sorry. It was my manager—
FAITH. That's okay. I thought I said something.
FREAK. No. I was being a dickhead. You didn't do anything.

FAITH. …Other than ordering a pizza. I did do that. *(A forced laugh.)*

FREAK. Yeah. *(Laughs.)* Veggie supreme. *(They laugh. Beat.)*

FAITH *(impressed he remembered)*. Yeah.

FREAK. Yeah…can I get you a Coke? My mom says Coke settles the stomach.

FAITH. So does mine…like who even knows if that like actually works…

FREAK. It also takes the paint off certain cars.

FAITH. What?

FREAK. Um…listen *(awkwardly)* …are you going to the prom?

FAITH *(beat)*. No.

FREAK. Do you want to go?

FAITH. Why are you asking me? We don't know each other. You don't know me…

FREAK. Do you think that's weird?

FAITH. Yes…but…

FREAK. Well?

FAITH. I mean, yes. I'll go.

FREAK. That's great. That's fuckin' great. *(He moves toward her.)*

FAITH. Oh, I just have to ask. I've got to run it by my mom, okay? Sorry, is that—

FREAK. Yeah, that's fine.

FAITH. Can I e-mail you?

FREAK. Sure, no problem. E-mail me. Just let me know.

FAITH. Okay. I'll e-mail you. *(He kisses her.)* Bye. *(As FAITH leaves the store, she looks up to God and freezes.)*

FREAK. All I want is to be surrounded by the flesh of a woman…someone who wanted to fuck like hell. Who can I trick into my room first? I can tell them what they want to hear, be all nice and sweet, and then tear their throat out with my teeth like a pop can, like a fucking wolf, show them who is God, oh, the lovely sounds of bones cracking and flesh ripping, Ahhh…

(FAITH unfreezes and exits.)

MANAGER VOICE. Okay, we need to talk.

FREAK. It's gone. I threw it out—

MANAGER VOICE. Do your parents know about this?

FREAK. No.

MANAGER VOICE. I think they should.

FREAK. Look, man, it's cool—

MANAGER VOICE. You think this is a joke? Get your keys. *(FREAK is silent, tension is building.)* We're going to your house and you can explain this to your parents…

FREAK. What?

MANAGER VOICE. Explain to them that I caught you at work…

FREAK. Jesus, no!

MANAGER VOICE. …shoving a pipe bomb up your ass. Now what would they say about that?

(FREAK stops, realizes the MANAGER has been teasing him.)

FREAK. Oh…fuck you. Fuck you.

MANAGER VOICE. You chicken shit… *(laughs)* you shoulda seen your face…white as a fuckin' ghost.

FREAK. Oh, you are an asshole, man. Don't do that.

MANAGER VOICE. Listen keep that shit out of the kitchen.

FREAK. Okay, thanks.

MANAGER VOICE. But something like this shouldn't go unpunished, so you get to close up.

FREAK. Oh thanks.

MANAGER VOICE. And do receipts. *(An afterthought.)* Pipe bombs. That's crazy.

(MANAGER exits. "You got mail" is heard. FREAK takes his apron off and goes to his computer.)

FREAK. Sweet!

(Projected is the e-mail. It slowly scrolls out.)

Hey, Pizza Man...I'm really sorry about this. I can't go. My mom said no. She thinks we don't know each other, and she's probably right. Plus, I probably should be going with this guy from youth group. I kinda told him yes already... It would've been fun. But let's hang out, Okay. Call me...

FREAK. Okay, I'll call you...you stuck-up little bitch, you fucking little Christianity godly whore.

(He slams the keyboard, as a sound of an I.M. is heard. Lights up on LONER, sitting at a computer with a large metal mixing bowl of cereal. Nothing is spoken unless otherwise indicated. The following dialogue is projected:)

I.M (Instant Messenger)

LONER (voDKa). sup nugget

FREAK (REB). sup

LONER (voDKa). what are you wearing

FREAK (REB). your mom

LONER (voDKa). you dirty bunny

FREAK (REB). stuck at work

LONER (voDKa). home bored

FREAK (REB). got caught w/ pipe bomb

FREAK (REB). must close shop.

FREAK (REB). pissed

FREAK (REB). !

LONER (voDKa) *(spoken)*. Shit. *(Typed.)* ☹*(Spoken.)* Awwww…

FREAK (REB). im serious. im fucking pissed.

LONER (voDKa). wanna see me draw an egg?

FREAK (REB). fuck off, stop it. i'm fucking stuck here.

LONER (voDKa). () *(types, presses return)* an egg.

FREAK (REB). fuckfuckfuck I wantout!!!!

LONER (voDKa). same. parents got a call… CW story was disturbing…

FREAK (REB). story?

LONER (voDKa). figure in black

LONER (voDKa). shooting preps

LONER (voDKa). carving flesh of jocks…

LONER (voDKa). nothing much

FREAK (REB) *(laughs)*. LOL u r a troubled little boy writing scary papers

LONER (voDKa). i made one of the pricks a little nervous

FREAK (REB). who?

LONER (voDKa). jockmutherfucker

FREAK (REB). prick fucked w/ me in gym
LONER (voDKa). prick dissed me in caf

*(Take a beat and the following two I.M.s appear simulta-
neously.)*

LONER (voDKa). what he do?
FREAK (REB). what did he do? *(Beat.)*
LONER (voDKa). talked shit.
FREAK (REB). yeah same.
FREAK (REB). what he say???
LONER (voDKa). some shit
LONER (voDKa). what HE say *(Long beat.)*
FREAK (REB). found my meds *(Beat.)*
LONER (voDKa). sorry
FREAK (REB). sorry for him...punched him in face. lots
of blood. taught him a lesson.
LONER (voDKa) *(spoken)*. Holy shit! *(Typed.)* FUCKIN
AWESOME!!!!!
FREAK (REB). not finished with him yet!
LONER (voDKa). cut off his cock feed it to his dog put it
in his mothers coffee microwave on high
FREAK (REB) *(spoken)*. What the— *(Typed.)* i smell a
plan
FREAK (REB). REVENGE??????????????????????????????
LONER (voDKa). FUCK YEAH! i'm serious! tonight...are
you in?
FREAK (REB). Reb is in.
FREAK (REB). is Vodka?
LONER (voDKa). AFFIRMATIVE!!!
FREAK (REB). DO WE HAVE AUDIO?
LONER *(spoken)*. We have audio.

FREAK. Video?

(They look behind them. Projected is a title card: RE-BEL MISSION, on fire.)

LONER & FREAK. Check!
FREAK. Then let's rock and roll.

MISCHIEF

(Energizing music sounds. While JOCK narrates, PER-FECT and FAITH dress FREAK. All of the actors nar-rate the scene as if they were sportscasters.)

ACTOR (Jock). Your name's Reb, short for Rebel. Why?
FREAK. It's the name of our high school mascot. He's a little Colonial soldier with a gun. Ready for a mission...

(While REBEL narrates, AP and PREP dress LONER.)

ACTOR (Rebel). Your name's Vodka. Why?
LONER. Drink of choice. Straight up...within an hour you're fucked. The shit you get into...
FREAK. Well, not by yourself. Adventure is never taken alone.
LONER. Never alone...
ACTOR (Perfect). Every rebel needs a mission...and a partner.
ACTOR (Faith). Someone who is creative, who inspires your mischievous mind...
ACTOR (AP). Who will execute your plans with the ut-most conviction...

ACTOR (Prep). Focused, determined, organized...

ALL. Wild, inventive, knows no bounds...

FREAK & LONER. The Adventures of...

FREAK. Reb & Vodka

LONER. Vodka & Reb

ACTOR (AP). Mission #1

ACTOR (Prep). Scene one...

ACTOR (All). Operation:

FREAK & LONER. Vengeance.

(The actors, reporters in a sport's telecast, stand to the sides and watch. Mission Impossible-esque theme music is heard as FREAK and LONER cross the stage. FREAK perches himself on a table.)

ACTOR (Perfect). Just look at Reb penetrate the outer perimeter and station himself on the shed of Target #1.

FREAK. A punk motherfucker who thought he was a bad-ass today...

ACTOR (Faith). One move and the Reb-man might ruin everything. But the patience. *(Watching FREAK.)* You just don't see this kind of disturbed intensity in today's youth.

LONER. Holy shit!

FREAK. What?

LONER. The Asshole's on his patio.

FREAK. Correction: the Target's in sight.

LONER. Out comes...

FREAK. Amanda.

(Company reacts, "Oh.")

LONER. Look at her sleek, black. Oh, she is a goddess.

FREAK *(to LONER)*. Ah, she is a paint gun.

ACTOR (Rebel). Hold everything... *(A light comes up center stage on a chair.)* Looks like an unattended white van has entered into the picture.

FREAK. That's what I'm seeing.

LONER. Unattended.

ACTOR (Jock). Rebel isn't the kind of player to let it just sit there undisturbed.

ACTOR (AP). Vodka will definitely want in on the action...

ACTOR (Perfect). But not without a plan. Rebel's too smart to go in without a plan.

FREAK. I'll be on lookout.

LONER. I'll smash the window.

(They approach the chair.)

ACTOR (Faith). Vodka seems to be hesitating. This kind of uncertainty may prove costly.

ACTOR (Rebel). The weapon:

LONER. A rock.

LONER. Is anyone coming...?

FREAK. Clear.

ALL. Smash!

LONER. Whoa! Oh God!

ACTOR (Jock). Reb is shaking!

FREAK. Like hell I am!

(LONER quickly runs to gather up what he can find in the car.)

ACTOR (Faith). The stolen goods:

LONER. Electrical stuff. And... *(looks to FREAK, holds up some "wires")* ...other things.

ACTOR (Prep). The alibi:

FREAK & LONER *(look to each other).* Uhhh...

ACTOR (Perfect). The getaway vehicle:

FREAK. My Honda. Ready.

ACTOR (Rebel). These boys can fly.

FREAK. Like lightning.

(The two arriving at another part of the stage, breathing heavily.)

ACTOR (Prep). Safe, parked few miles from the scene.

ACTOR (Faith). What a night.

ACTOR (Jock). What a high.

ACTORS (All). What a team.

LONER. Reb and Vodka.

FREAK. Vodka and Reb.

LONER. No longer captives to their progressive pretentious Little Town.

FREAK. No longer bound by the rules.

LONER. Above the law.

FREAK & LONER. I am the law!

FREAK. Superhero.

LONER. Superhuman.

LONER & FREAK. Natural selection, baby.

(Police lights flash, sirens sound, a spotlight shines on them. They turn toward the light. As the siren dies, they turn toward the audience. Lights move to two separate spots on the boys. The voice of a JUDGE is heard.)

JUDGE (Prep). To the charge of first-degree criminal tres-
pass, theft and criminal mischief. What is your plea?

FREAK. Guilty.

LONER. Guilty.

JUDGE (Prep). First time out of the box and you get
caught? I don't believe it. It's a rare occurrence when
someone gets caught their first time. It is the verdict of
this court that the defendants serve one year in the juvenile diversion program. I hope your parents' eyes are finally open.

(Sound of a gavel smashing down.)

DINNER

*(The actors cross to tables upstage. Lights on FREAK's
dinner table. REBEL is his mother, JOCK is his father.
FREAK's father is severe and implacable. His mother is
cautious and compliant.)*

MOTHER *(So how do we approach this...)*. Well...

FATHER *(We're not going to talk about it)*. What a day!

MOTHER *(trying to open the door again)*. I don't know.

FATHER *(Fine. Let's talk)*. What?

MOTHER *(emotional, confused)*. Why would he—

FATHER *(dismissive, I have this under control)*. Don't
worry.

MOTHER *(It's not my place)*. Okay.

*(FREAK enters. He is cautious and respectful with his
father, loving with his mother.)*

FATHER *(doesn't look up from the plate, neutral)*. Hey.
MOTHER *(loving)*. Hi.
FREAK *(responding to his mother, worried about his father)*. Hey.
MOTHER *(anything but the tension in the room)*. Want some?
FREAK *(appreciative)*. Thanks.
MOTHER *(really asking)*. How are—
FREAK *(distracted by his father's silence)*. Fine.

(MOTHER exits.)

FATHER *(unaffected)*. School?
FREAK *(trying to comply)*. Fine. Work?
FATHER. Fine. Work?
FREAK. Same.

(MOTHER re-enters with plate.)

MOTHER. Here.
FREAK *(welcome relief)*. Thanks. *(Beat.)*
FATHER *(putting the fork down. He is ready to talk)*. Well?

(Long pause. FREAK stares at his plate.)

MOTHER *(Before your father explodes)*. Say something?
FREAK *(genuine; realizing the massive amount of trouble he is in)*. I'm sorry.
FATHER *(shocked with the brevity)*. I'm sorry?
FREAK *(I really truly am, Dad)*. Yeah.
FATHER *(That's all you can muster?)*. That's all—
FREAK *(not knowing what's expected of him)*. I'm going...

MOTHER *(worried about him)*. Where?

FREAK *(frustrated with the situation)*. Out.

FATHER *(starts to eat again, unaffected)*. Not tonight.

FREAK *(You obviously don't want me here)*. Why?

FATHER *(I don't need to explain anything to you, unaffected)*. No.

FREAK *(What do you want from me?)*. Come on.

FATHER *(glares at him, straining not to explode)*. Enough. *(Beat.)*

FREAK *(attempting to comply)*. How long?

FATHER *(unaffected, he got his way)*. Two months.

FREAK *(challenging)*. For what?

FATHER *(You really want me to answer this)*. For what?

FREAK *(It was stupid, I didn't rob a bank)*. For nothing.

FATHER *(disgusted with him)*. NOTHING!

FREAK *(defiant)*. I'm going...

FATHER *(Do you think you have any say in this?)*. Where?

FREAK *(Where you've confined me)*. My room.

MOTHER *(trying to help)*. Finish your—

FREAK *(trying not to cry. We're not a family)*. Why?

FATHER *(back to his dinner. He's doing what I want)*. Let him go.

FREAK *(didn't want it to end this way)*. Thanks.

(FREAK pushes his chair under the table and exits. Lights up on LONER's family, R of FREAK's: FAITH is his mother, AP is his father. LONER's father is introverted, hesitant and slightly distant. His mother is organized, efficient and driving her husband. LONER enters. He says the bare minimum and avoids the problem.)

FATHER *(wanting everything normal)*. Hey.

MOTHER *(letting her son know that things aren't all right)*. Hi.

LONER *(unaffected)*. Hey.

MOTHER *(Clearly something needs to be said)*. Want some?

LONER *(unaffected)*. Thanks.

MOTHER *(Are you going to say something?)*. How are—

LONER *(stops it from going there)*. Fine.

(MOTHER looks to FATHER to start the conversation before she exits.)

FATHER *(trying to start a conversation)*. School?

LONER *(This conversation is ridiculous)*. Fine. Work?

FATHER. Fine. Work?

LONER *(almost disgusted with his father's approach)*. Same.

(MOTHER re-enters with plate.)

MOTHER *(practical)*. Here.

LONER *(trying to be civil)*. Thanks.

(Beat. MOTHER stares at FATHER until he speaks.)

FATHER *(doesn't look at LONER)*. Well?

(Long pause. LONER keeps eating.)

MOTHER *(puts it out on the table)*. Say something!

LONER *(What do you want me to say?)*. I'm sorry.

FATHER *(confirming it)*. I'm sorry?

LONER *(Am I going to say "I'm not"?)*. Yeah.

FATHER *(Then that's all that needs to be said)*. That's
    all—

LONER *(This conversation is ridiculous)*. I'm going...

MOTHER *(We're not done yet)*. Where?

LONER *(Where else?)*. Out.

FATHER *(getting a look from his wife)*. Not tonight.

LONER *(There's more to this...)*. Why?

FATHER *(not wanting to come down hard)*. No.

LONER *(This is bullshit)*. Come on.

FATHER *(Please don't force me into this situation)*.
    Enough.

LONER *(I can't believe this)*. How long?

FATHER *(checking with his wife; this seems fair)*. Two
    months.

LONER *(This isn't that big of a deal)*. For what?

FATHER *(Son, this is a big deal)*. For what?

LONER *(I didn't do anything serious)*. For nothing.

FATHER *(looks to his wife: I don't have the words to ex-
    plain this to him)*. NOTHING!

LONER *(I don't respect you)*. I'm going...

FATHER *(trying to be a father again)*. Where?

LONER *(biting; at his mother since she put his father up
    to this)*. My room.

MOTHER *(putting her foot down)*. Finish your—

LONER *(ignoring, purposefully walking away)* Why?

FATHER *(No more fighting, please)*. Let him go.

LONER *(walking away)*. Thanks.

*(LONER exits. Lights come up on FREAK's family, as
LONER's continues to eat.)*

LONER'S MOTHER. I don't understand.

FREAK'S FATHER. I don't understand.

FREAK'S MOTHER. This anger…

LONER'S MOTHER. What's going on with him?

LONER'S FATHER. It's that school.

FREAK'S FATHER. It's that computer.

FREAK'S MOTHER. Why would he push us away?

LONER'S MOTHER. Why won't he let us in?

FREAK'S FATHER *(to the spouse)*. You try talking to him.

LONER'S MOTHER. You're his…

ALL. Mother/Father…

FREAK'S MOTHER. He hates me.

LONER'S FATHER. He loves you.

LONER'S MOTHER. I hated my father.

LONER'S FATHER. I talked to my mother.

FREAK'S FATHER. It's just a phase…

LONER'S MOTHER. He's a boy.

FREAK'S MOTHER. He's just a boy.

LONER'S FATHER. …who's into violence.

FREAK'S FATHER. I was into violence.

LONER'S MOTHER. Does he need help?

FREAK'S MOTHER. He has help.

LONER'S MOTHER. Some medication…

FREAK'S FATHER. He has medication…

LONER'S MOTHER. Someone to talk to?

LONER'S FATHER. He has someone to talk to…

ALL. Us. *(Beat.)* Us?

FREAK'S MOTHER. What can we do?

LONER'S MOTHER. What can I do?

FATHERS. Try talking to him.

MOTHERS. I have.

LONER'S MOTHER. He doesn't want to talk.
LONER'S FATHER. I was like that too...
FREAK'S FATHER. Give him space.
LONER'S MOTHER. And time...
FREAK'S MOTHER. He's a good kid.
FREAK'S FATHER. He'll talk...
LONER'S FATHER. When he's ready...
LONER'S MOTHER. He'll have something to say... *(Beat.)*
ALL. What will he have to say?

(Lights up on PERFECT, looking out to audience. She is talking to her mother. She oscillates between having no respect for her mother and needing some advice.)

PERFECT. If I told you...what would you say? *(Beat.)* Maybe you know. Maybe you don't. Maybe you should...
MOTHERS *(spoken by the boys' mothers frozen at the dinner table).* Something.
PERFECT. Remember Steve? You loved him. You loved how he smiled and sat across from you at this very table. Do you know that Steve laughs at you?—laughs that you drive a bus? I heard him laugh one night about the white-trash school-bus driver...and even I laughed. Do you know he spent the night? I was in bed and he knocked on my window...I knew you were upstairs. Yeah...I thought about waking you but, c'mon what would I have said? Could you imagine, me sitting on your comforter naked, his beer on my breath, asking you, "Is this the right time to do it?" Yeah...what would you have told me?
MOTHERS. Something.

PERFECT. So, Mother, it just kind of happened. He was so into it and I don't think he heard me... I said no, but he said it was all right, so I guess it was okay, but...it hurt and I asked him to...but he looked at me really like intensely...and after a while he put his clothes on and left...and... *(Beat.)* I mean it can't be, Mom, if he's my boyfriend, and we love each other, I mean it's not like he can... If he's my boyfriend... I mean it's not his fault if I let him in the window and...well, you could have heard him? Maybe you did, but you didn't want to bother me...wanted to give me my space. You are always good about that, Mom...

MOTHERS. Something?

PERFECT. It was fine...next time it will be better. I know that. You've gotta experience these things to know. Yeah...

(Music fades in.[2])

MOTHERS. Was there something you wanted to tell me?

PERFECT. No. It was nothing.

(Lights fade as the cast prepares for ALONE. The music fades in stronger. The cast lines up upstage and in unison, slam the doors of their respective bedrooms and take their places on stage. The music swells. They are unaware of one another, alone.)

---

2 "Bittersweet Symphony" was used in the original production. Permission must be obtained from the copyright holder.

ALONE

(The action set out below should be underscored and consistently punctuated by the song chosen to underscore it. The effect of ALONE, which moves from character to character, is that of a music video. In the original production, "Bittersweet Symphony" by The Verve was used, and the lyrics corresponded to the actors' actions as they were each illuminated—so much so that the cast sung the lyrics in their respective moments. However, should the producing theatre company be unable to obtain permission to use the song, an effective substitute should be chosen. What's critical is that the lyrics of the song reflect the emotional state of each character and continues to tell the story of their personal strife. The actors never acknowledge each other throughout.

Moment 1: A tableau of all of the adolescents, alone, having just closed their bedroom door.

Moment 2: Adolescents travel to their bedroom and begin their respective activity.

Moment 3: Lights to LONER who sits beside his bed. He writes in his journal. After a moment of writing, he pierces the journal with his pencil in frustration.

Moment 4: Lights switch to AP, sitting at a desk with a huge SAT practice book in front of his face. He sets the book down and stares at a clock timer. He picks up his pencil. Staring at the clock, hits the top to start it ticking, and then starts to write.

Moment 5: REBEL is now lit, pushing her sleeves up.

Moment 6: Lights out on AP. REBEL takes out an Ex-act-o knife. She turns away as she begins to make little cuts in her arm.

Moment 7: Lights switch solely to JOCK, who tosses his shirt. He stares at his body. He goes into a sit up posi-tion. He starts a long series of sit-ups. Faster and faster and collapses.

Moment 8: Lights switch to PERFECT, looking in a mir-ror (the audience). She lifts her shirt enough to expose her stomach. Then pulls her stomach in and releases. She lifts a toilet seat.

Moment 9: FAITH is lit, on her knees with a rosary blessing herself, as PERFECT drops to her knees. Lights out on PERFECT as she starts to vomit.

Moment 10: FAITH stands and picks up her prom dress, places it against her body.

Moment 11: As she lets the dress drop, lights switch to PREP, at a mirror. He is looking at himself, as he messes hair. He stops and stares, disgusted by what he sees.

Moment 12: Lights switch to FREAK, sitting in front of his computer. He is wildly playing a video game.

Moment 13: As FREAK tosses the joystick, lights come up on everyone moving around their rooms in frustration.

Moment 14: Lights switch to REBEL who has just cut her arms several times in self-mutilation. She hangs off her bed, as blood runs down her arm.

Moment 15: Lights switch to LONER, as he tears up his journal and takes out a pipe bomb from his backpack. He looks to be sure no one is entering the room.

Moment 16: Lights switch to FAITH, dancing with her prom dress as a partner.

Moment 17: Lights switch to PERFECT looking at a pregnancy test. She waits, and then discovers she is pregnant.

Moment 18: Lights switch to AP who writes, checks the clock, writes, checks the clock, writes. This increases in speed, until he tears his practice test.

Moment 19: Lights switch to JOCK, punching the air wildly.

Moment 20: Lights switch to FREAK, standing on a chair panning the room with a TEC-9 semiautomatic.

Moment 21: Lights switch to PREP looking in the mirror, as he is putting on black eyeliner.

Moment 22: ALL are lit. FREAK and LONER jump off their chairs, AP flings the book off his desk and throws the timer, PREP throws the eyeliner and wipes his make-up off, JOCK collapses, PERFECT throws the pregnancy test, FAITH tosses the dress, REBEL throws the knife. All of them crawl into fetal positions facing downstage. They all experience a moment of pain and loneliness.

Moment 23: FREAK and LONER slowly stand across the stage facing each other.

(The music should be at its climax. They acknowledge each other, then turn upstage and out of light.)

Moment 24: All actors except FREAK and LONER come downstage hiding FREAK AND LONER as they lay their signature props in their original positions and exit.

Moment 25: FREAK and LONER cross downstage into the light. They are now wearing black trenchcoats. As the music starts to fade, they look to each other, then look to the audience and smile. Blackout. The music trails off...)

END OF ACT I

ACT II

(Stage and houselights are up. Laid out on two chairs are the second-act costumes for the roles of ERIC HARRIS and DYLAN KLEBOLD. DYLAN's costume: a black T-shirt with the words "Wrath" written in red, a Boston Red Sox hat, with the "B" only on the backside, a small silver ring with a black oval, and a trench coat. ERIC's costume: a white T-shirt with the words "Natural Selection" written in black, a digital watch, black webbing for ammunition, and a trench coat. These were the actual clothes of the two killers on the day of the shootings.

On a table are laid out two guns: a TEC-9 and a sawed-off shotgun, a prescription bottle of Luvox, a 1998 camcorder, and a bottle of Jack Daniels. On the other table are the following: a computer keyboard, a can of Coke, a stack of pipe bombs, Molotov cocktails, crickets, a black toolbox [containing pliers, three black dual bell-and-clacker alarm clocks with removable backs, and extra wiring], Eric's day planner and a pencil, and the camcorder case. All the props are replicas of the actual props found in Eric's bedroom.

The actors playing FREAK and LONER enter and lay down on the deck. Music: "How to Disappear Completely" by Radiohead[3] is heard. Lights fade to black.)

DYLAN & ERIC

(Note: This scene is the transformation from the two actors playing FREAK and LONER into ERIC HARRIS and DYLAN KLEBOLD. The actors approach the scene knowing the journey they are about to take. There is an element of resistance in the scene that eventually fades into inevitability. They are not eager to put on these clothes, but it is their duty and responsibility in telling this story. The scene is ritualistic and genuine, with absolutely no air of pretense or affectation.

Projected in the darkness are the graduation photos of Dylan Klebold and Eric Harris.

Lights come up on the actors playing FREAK and LONER as they stare at the photos, then look to each other and cross to the clothing. They contemplate putting on the clothes, then turn to the props. They examine the guns and pipe bombs. As they pick up a pipe bomb and a gun respectively...

Projected: Photos of DYLAN and ERIC from the day of the shootings. The actors look to each other, put down their weapons and begin to dress.

---

3 Used in the original production. Permission must be obtained from the copyright holder.

Once completed, they look to each other, move to their chairs, and lights and sound cut out as they sit on opposite sides of the stage from each other. They face the audience, and never acknowledge each other. Their transformation is complete.)

JUVENILE DIVERSION

("Session 1: April 14, 1998" projected.)

VOICE (Rebel & Prep). State your name.

DYLAN. Dylan Bennett Klebold

ERIC. Eric David Harris

VOICE (Both). And you attend Columbine High School?

DYLAN & ERIC. Yes.

VOICE (Both). And you live in Littleton?

DYLAN & ERIC *(not in unison)*. Yes.

VOICE (Both). All your life?

DYLAN. Yes.

ERIC. No.

VOICE (Prep). Explain.

ERIC. I moved from Plattsburgh, New York…actually I was born in Wichita, moved to Ohio, Michigan, then to Plattsburgh. We moved to Littleton when I was in 7th grade.

VOICE (Prep). Lots of moving… Dad in the military?

ERIC. Yeah, he was.

VOICE (Rebel). Okay, Dylan, describe what happened.

DYLAN. I…I wrote all this down.

VOICE (Rebel). I'd like to hear it from you.

DYLAN. I broke into a van. Took stuff from it. Drove away (friend's car). Cops discovered us. Admitted to the crime.

ERIC. I broke into a car and stole $1700 worth of equipment, was caught thirty minutes later.

VOICE (Prep). And what do you make of your punishment?

ERIC. Do I like it?

VOICE (Rebel). Instead of jail time you'll be meeting with me. I mean, you must have some reaction to that.

DYLAN. I'm hoping I can get the best I can out of it and am optimistic about it. So far it sucks.

ERIC *(suppressing anger)*. Looking forward to it. Hopefully it will set me straight.

VOICE (Prep). Do you feel you've gotten on the wrong path?

ERIC *(impatient)*. Yes. Clearly, I mean—well, clearly it's what you all think. *(Beat.)*

VOICE (Both). And what does your family think?

DYLAN. Oh, they were thrilled. *(Sincere.)* They were devastated.

ERIC. Shocked them. All trust is lost.

VOICE (Both). Would you say this has been one of the most traumatic experiences in your life?

DYLAN. Yes.

ERIC. Yes. And moving from Plattsburgh.

VOICE (Rebel). Now, what's your relationship with the co-defendant?

DYLAN. Co-defendant?

ERIC. He's my best friend...past and current.

DYLAN. We've been friends for about four years. Very good friends.

VOICE (Rebel). How do you spend your free time?

DYLAN. Spend most of my time at home. In my room. Alone. This is where you note that I'm anti-social...

VOICE (Rebel). I want you to tell me what's going on. Look on that sheet and tell me which of the following you are having problems or difficulty with...

(The boys' checklists are projected. The lines are checked off as the boys fill out the forms.)

DYLAN *(looks at the sheet and checks as he reads off)*. Finances and jobs.

ERIC. Anger, anxiety, authority figures, depression, disorganized thoughts, homicidal thoughts, jealousy, loneliness, mood swings, obsessive thoughts, racing thoughts, stress, suspiciousness...oh, and... *(a final check)* ...temper.

VOICE (Rebel). Do you want to explain?

DYLAN. It's kind of difficult to find a technician job when I am only sixteen years old.

VOICE (Rebel). Very funny, wise guy.

VOICE (Prep). Eric? Please, could you try and explain?

ERIC. I... *(Beat. A sincere, but difficult attempt to open up.)* Sometimes I get so angry. I punch walls.

VOICE (Prep). Go on.

ERIC. I've got this short temper, often get angry at almost anything I don't like.

VOICE (Both). Do you feel in control of your life?

DYLAN. Yes.

ERIC. Yes.

VOICE (Both). Have you ever used drugs?

DYLAN. Drugs are a waste of everything. Definitely not worth it. My brother, case in point...

ERIC. I'm on medication, I told you. Anti-depressants. I've
    had drinks, smoked pot, but I don't need that anymore.

VOICE (Both). And are you sexually active?

DYLAN. I'm...

ERIC. Oh...

DYLAN & ERIC. No.

VOICE (Both). Have you ever been sexually active?

ERIC. No. I told you— Jesus. No. No. No.

DYLAN. Nope. Uh-uh. God...

VOICE (Both). Are you both versed in sexual education—

DYLAN & ERIC *(overlapping)*. Yes, yes—oh, God, of
    course, yes...

VOICE (Rebel) *(smiling)*. Okay, okay.

*(They move closer but still do not acknowledge each
other. DYLAN is resisting the counselor; ERIC is now
playing the game.*

"Session 2: July 10, 1998" projected.)

VOICE (Rebel). So what do you think of your Diversion
    classes?

ERIC. The anger management class I took was helpful in
    many ways. If a person does not want to control his or
    her anger, then it can be a problem.

VOICE (Rebel). Dylan?

DYLAN. Truthfully?

VOICE (Rebel). Yes.

DYLAN. It wasn't worth my time.

VOICE (Rebel). What do you mean?

DYLAN. It was an eight-hour day of pointless review and
    cramped conditions. I feel that I shouldn't have had to

take that class, but I'm just trying to get out of the diversion program.

VOICE (Rebel). Well, if you've already embraced the class's message, your progress report isn't showing it. A "D" in math and composition—and your teacher reports that you are sleeping in math class...

DYLAN. I'm only sleeping in class because I was up the night before doing an essay—

VOICE (Both). If you want to get through this process, no more excuses.

(DYLAN and ERIC look at each other in agreement.)

ERIC. It won't happen again.
DYLAN. I promise.

(They move their chairs next to each other. Both of them are excellent actors and maintain the exact level of believability needed to fool their counselors.

"Session 3: January 19, 1999" projected.)

VOICE (Prep). And tell me again why I am seeing you together today?

DYLAN. I thought my dentist's appointment was in the morning—

ERIC. But it wasn't. Dylan messed up the time, so I told him to come to my two-thirty appointment.

VOICE (Prep). Ah, ha. In the future, I'd prefer to see the two of you apart.

ERIC & DYLAN. Oh yes. Of course, right.

DYLAN. You'll note my grades are improving...

VOICE (Prep). Except that D in calculus and an F in gym...

ERIC. Yes, but look at my three A's...

VOICE (Prep). I see...

DYLAN. I'm working for my next-door neighbor doing yard work and landscaping...

VOICE (Prep). Good. Very good.

ERIC. And I've changed my meds...my mood is improving and I feel better.

DYLAN. Most importantly...

ERIC. I am truly sorry for what I have done.

DYLAN. I know what I did was wrong.

VOICE (Prep & Rebel). I placed a call to your parents to discuss early termination, and they have no problems with my decision.

DYLAN. Thanks. Thank you very much.

ERIC *(overlapping)*. That's great—I really appreciate that. Thank you.

(ERIC and DYLAN look to each other and smile. Lights to black. Projected are the final reports of the Diversion counselors, as they are read.)

VOICE (Prep). Eric did a very nice job on Diversion. He is a very bright young man who is likely to succeed in life. Seems responsible and remorseful. He suffers from depression but has changed his meds and feels better. He says he has difficulties handling stress, but says he has a good handle on it now. He impressed me as being very articulate and intelligent.

(Lights on ERIC, sitting on a table holding a video camera. This is a video journal entry.)

ERIC. Well, folks, today was a very important day in the history of Reb. Today, I got a double-barrel 12-gauge shotgun, a pump-action 12-gauge shotgun, and a 9mm carbine. It's all over now; this is point of no return. Well, I've gotta get that Marine application out before they start with me. *(Beat.)* It's weird, I don't feel like punching through a door anymore.

(Projected: "January 14, 1999: File Closed."

ERIC turns the camera off.)

VOICE (Prep). January 14, 1999: File closed.
VOICE (Rebel). Dylan is a bright young man who has a great deal of potential. If he is able to tap his potential and become self-motivated he should do well in life. I also confronted him on his minimizing and excuse giving. It all sounds like he feels like the victim although he denies this. All in all: Nice young man, kind of goofy, and a bizarre sense of humor, he makes me laugh.

(Lights on DYLAN, sitting on a table holding a video camera. This is a video journal entry.)

DYLAN. I just got back from Arizona. Can you believe it? Touring a college with my dad...it was cool. But they have no clue. Days from now the judgment will begin.

It's interesting knowing I'm going to die…everything
has a touch of triviality to it.

(Projected: "March 3, 1999: File Closed.")

VOICE (Rebel). March 3, 1999: File closed.

(DYLAN turns the camera off.

*On the slate is projected the display of a video camera.
It is dated March 15, 1999. Standby symbol flashes.)*

ERIC. Ready?
DYLAN. Ready.

*(Standby goes to Record, as the lights snap up. DYLAN
is recording ERIC. They are in his bedroom.)*

THE BASEMENT TAPES

ERIC. Okay, it's about 1:30 a.m. Less than forty-eight
hours to Judgment Day. We want to take you on a tour
of what we've been up to over the last few months.
DYLAN. We've been busy little beavers.
ERIC. That's Vodka on camera. Say hello, Vodka?
DYLAN. Hello Vodka…
ERIC. Welcome to the arsenal of freedom. Better known as
my bedroom. My parents are a bit too trusting.
DYLAN. Ah, they're clueless.
ERIC. Yeah, Green Mountain Guns called the other day
and my dad answered the phone. They're like "Your

clips are in." My dad says, "I didn't order any clips."
Fucking hysterical...

DYLAN. We were this close from being fucked.

ERIC. Anyway, they don't come in here. I keep it clean.
They stay out. Okay, here we have the Delta batch—

DYLAN. Created by yours truly.

ERIC. And we've got a pretty awesome supply of crickets
and pipe bombs. These are for the first ten minutes.
Smoke 'em out. Scare 'em out. Then Molotov's if we
get bored, mix and match...

DYLAN. But the real stars of the show... *(Hands off the camera.)*

ERIC. Drum roll...

DYLAN *(picks up the guns).* Arlene *(shotgun)* and Sam-
antha *(TEC-9)* —she's a feisty one! Brought to us by
Mr. Mark Ma—

ERIC *(censoring him).* Mr. John Doe.

DYLAN. Yeah...

ERIC. And a certain girlfriend of a certain mass murderer—

DYLAN. A prom date does not constitute a girlfriend.

ERIC. —who bought us these little babies. Dylan will see
to a very personal thank you...

DYLAN. Fuck you.

ERIC. Anyway, guys, we hope you don't get any shit for
buying us these.

DYLAN. Yeah, we're sorry about that. But it was our
choice, our doing.

(ERIC puts down the camera in front of him to free his hands.)

ERIC. And for you other motherfuckers, don't blame the gun shows or any other stores for selling us shit because it's not their fault.

DYLAN. Yeah, I don't want no fucking laws on buying fucking PVC pipes.

ERIC. Go ahead and change the gun laws—

DYLAN *(interrupting)*. How do you think we got ours?

ERIC. And don't blame the school—

DYLAN. Yeah, the administration is doing a fine job as it is.

ERIC. We are kind of a select case here, so don't think this will happen again.

DYLAN. We're not like those kids in Arkansas. Idiots got caught.

ERIC. I hope you realize what we are implying here. The most deaths in U.S. history.

DYLAN. Yeah, the police, parents, the world will be studying these videos.

ERIC. Thinking why? Why would they do such a thing?

DYLAN. Maybe they felt helpless, hopeless, alone?

ERIC *(pushing DYLAN out of the camera; DYLAN gets a Coke from the table)*. It's hatred that fuels this fire. See, even you are hating us right now. But I'll tell you something. You made me. You made US. *(Flipping an obscene gesture toward the camera.)* Look at what you made. You're fucking shit, you humans, and you need to die. Even us. We need to die too of course. We'll fuckin' die killing you fuckin' shits. It's war. And in war there are victims. We...the victims. *(Into the camera.)* But this...all of this is the end of that. *(Close to the camera.)* I have so much rage inside me. Worst than a loaded gun because you just don't expect anything vis-

cous from silence. Silence is deadly. The longer the silence, the more deadly. Shhhhhhh! *(As he says this, he
grows quieter and quieter.)* BANG!

(DYLAN startled, knocks over the Coke.)

ERIC. You idiot!
DYLAN. Sorry, man...
ERIC. What the hell, Dylan! That's all I need is a disaster
on the floor and my mom will start. I need things in or-
der here.
DYLAN. Okay.
ERIC. In fucking order...
DYLAN. Sorry.
ERIC. Turn the fucking camera off.

*(Awkward silence. DYLAN turns off the camera. The
stage goes to black, as static is projected on the slate.)*

WHAT IF

*(Lights fade up on DYLAN, lying on the table next to the
Jack, playing with the TEC-9. ERIC is sitting at his
computer typing. His e-mail is projected, as we hear his
typing. He does not speak this aloud:)*

By now it's over. If you are reading this, my mission is
complete. Your children who have ridiculed me, who
have chosen not to accept me are dead. Surely you will
try to blame it on the clothes I wear, the music I listen
to—but no: parents and teachers, YOU have taught these
kids to be gears and sheep. I may have taken their lives

and my own—but LET THIS MASSACRE BE ON YOUR SHOULDERS UNTIL THE DAY YOU DIE. I did not choose this life, but I have indeed chosen to exit it. You may think the horror ends with the bullet in my head—but all that I will leave you with is to decipher what more extensive death is to come. Reb.

DYLAN. So this is a bizarre question, but how do you really think it will end?

ERIC. Well, we're not getting out of there alive—not with all those cops out there. So, the best way to go is a shootout.

DYLAN. And then?

ERIC. Then what? We're dead. We're history...the greatest school shooting of all time.

DYLAN. And after that?

ERIC. What do you mean, "after that"?

DYLAN. Oh, come on...like you haven't thought about this.

ERIC. What is there to think about?

DYLAN. We're going to be dead in two days.

ERIC. Yeah, it's weird knowing you are going to die.

DYLAN. Weird? It's terrifying.

ERIC. Yeah, that's the best part.

DYLAN. Oh yeah...like you're not a bit scared.

ERIC. Look, why we are even talking about this?

DYLAN. Dude, why are you so sensitive?

ERIC. Okay, Dylan, let's talk about death. The afterlife, if there is one, is like the final level of Doom, okay? Destroying, killing—

DYLAN. Fucking Doom?

ERIC. It's blackness. It's nothing. It's just over.

DYLAN. How do you know?

ERIC. I know.

DYLAN. No. You can't know. No one knows. You just too scared to think about it?

ERIC. Look, we have always been set on this. We put guns to our heads and count one, two, three. That is the plan. It is what I will do. And I need you to do it, too. Like we planned. Over and over, now what the fuck?

DYLAN. You just think you're going to be able to kill yourself just like that? Bang and that's it?

ERIC. There's no thinking. You're gonna have blood on your hands from these guns. The kickback is going to destroy your hands. You won't be thinking about anything. Your heart will be pounding and the gun will be the only thing you can do.

DYLAN. Okay, I hear you. You're in my face here.

ERIC. Good, because you don't have a choice. Gun in hand, I will end my life and you will end yours. End of discussion.

DYLAN *(beat)*. What if I don't?

ERIC. What did you say?

DYLAN. What if you shoot first, but I decide not to? What are you gonna do then?

ERIC. What is this? You want to fuck this up? I'm not gonna let you fuck this up. You're out. Get the fuck out. Get out. *(DYLAN goes.)* Okay, Dylan you're going. Okay. Yeah. Hey, you forgot your camera. *(DYLAN goes to get the camera.)* What the hell? What's your problem? Christ… *(ERIC crosses to the window and grabs his arm.)*

DYLAN. What's your problem? I asked you a simple question—

ERIC. Two days before? You wait until tonight to ask your simple question?

DYLAN. Fine, no more questions. I'll just do what I'm told and not say a thing.

ERIC. Sit the fuck down.

DYLAN. I'll pretend that I'm not scared and run around here giving orders like some fucking Marine.

ERIC. WHAT THE FUCK DO YOU KNOW ABOUT THE MARINES? *(Goes after him, knocking him to the ground; turns the safety off on the shotgun; points it at his face.)* Jesus Christ, you asshole. You have no idea what I'm capable of. *(Drops the gun and moves away.)*

DYLAN. You are fucked, man. Fucked. *(ERIC turns away.)* Why would you do that? Why would you fucking do that to me?

ERIC *(starts to break down)*. Fuck you. You're such an asshole...

DYLAN. What, the Marines?

ERIC. Well, that's it, eh?

DYLAN. Oh.

ERIC. My parents are fucking idiots. *(Tries to laugh.)*

DYLAN. What'd they do—

ERIC. The Marines don't take drugs, Mom, not even prescription...

DYLAN. She told the recruiter?

ERIC *(moves on)*. It doesn't matter.

DYLAN. They didn't let you in because of a prescription drug?

ERIC. It doesn't matter.

DYLAN. I'm sorry—

ERIC *(erupts)*. Jesus Christ, you asshole.

DYLAN. What—

ERIC. What do you want, Dylan? You want to live this fucking life? I'm done. Okay? I want one last memory. One I've been planning more than trying to finger your little girlfriend at the prom...

DYLAN. She's not my girlfriend, you fuck. She is a friend that went to the prom with your friend who happened to buy us these guns. What's your problem?

ERIC. I wouldn't know, Dylan. I sat here stuffing pipe bombs all night. Tell me what prom was like. I don't know. *(ERIC jumps right back to previous discussion without a beat.)* Go on. You can lick smelly ass until the day we throw our little caps in the air and sing "Columbine. Oh Columbine"? And Miss Valedictory gives her prize-winning speech about how wonderful it was at Columbine High School, all the friends she made...when you and I and maybe four others out of a class of what, 350, actually talked to her? I'm not going to sit there to listen to bullshit spew from what is supposed to be the smartest person in the class...fuck me. No way. They don't deserve that day. They don't deserve one more day past Tuesday. I want them to feel they almost got away with it. One last prom. One last yearbook picture...

DYLAN. You're not taking it, are you?

ERIC. What?

DYLAN *(picks up the bottle)*. Your medicine. You're pretty fucked up...

ERIC. What...you're worried 'cause I'm angry?

DYLAN *(tosses the bottle at him)*. I mean, look at you...

ERIC. Don't fuck with me, Dylan.

DYLAN. You can't even stand still.

ERIC. Shut the fuck up.

DYLAN. Is all this in your plan?

ERIC. You are a sad, lanky, ugly loner—
DYLAN. …WHO WENT TO THE FUCKING PROM.
   (ERIC doesn't know what to do; DYLAN waits.) It's a
   real surprise the Marines didn't want to add a bi-polar
   freak to their ranks—

   *(ERIC punches him. DYLAN throws ERIC to the ground
   and eventually punches him in the face.)*

ERIC. Stop. Stop. FUCK!
DYLAN *(full of rage mixed with pain. Seeing ERIC's nose
   bleeding).* Jesus fucking Christ, Eric. Why do you have
   to push this? You keep pushing…
ERIC. I'm sorry.
DYLAN. Fuck. I didn't want to hit you. I didn't want all
   this.
ERIC. You didn't want all this?
DYLAN. No. I don't know. I wanted this, but I didn't
   want…
ERIC. What?
DYLAN. I don't want to fight you. I don't hate you. It's
   about *them*.
ERIC. That's why we're doing this.
DYLAN. Then what the fuck is our problem. Let's just do
   it.
ERIC. Okay, okay. It is going to happen. That's why that
   closet's full of pipe bombs…
DYLAN. I want them to pay.
ERIC. And these guns are real.
DYLAN. I wanna watch them pay.
ERIC. And Reb is fucking real, man. And so is Vodka.

DYLAN. I want them to feel this...like a knife to the skin of America, slicing her, with a jagged edge. The skin's bunched up, digs in deep. It won't heal without a scar.

ERIC. Right here, man. *(Handing him the gun.)* Right here. We'll leave a scar on America that will never heal. We're gonna kick start a revolution. We'll be remembered forever. Like gods, man, like fucking gods...

DYLAN. Directors will die to film this movie.

ERIC. They'll be fighting over us.

DYLAN. Spielberg or Tarantino?

ERIC & DYLAN. FUCKING TARANTINO.

DYLAN. And of course they'll blame the movies.

ERIC. But who actually blows up their school?

DYLAN. No one. Just us.

ERIC. Planned to the "T."

DYLAN. Executed without error.

ERIC. All right here. *(Picks up his day planner.)* Five a.m.?

DYLAN. We get up.

ERIC. No big deal because of...

DYLAN. Tuesday-morning bowling.

ERIC. Six a.m.?

DYLAN. We arrive at Littleton Lanes and bowl just like normal.

ERIC. STRIIIKE!!!

ERIC & DYLAN. Heil Hitler!

ERIC. Seven a.m.?

DYLAN. Back to your house.

ERIC. Load up the car.

DYLAN. Your parents at work.

ERIC. Eight-thirty a.m.?

DYLAN. Back to my house. Set up the car.

ERIC. *Your* parents at work.

ERIC. Ten-thirty a.m.?

DYLAN. The decoy...

ERIC. Two backpacks with pipe bombs...

DYLAN. ...and propane tanks...

ERIC. ...placed in an open space three miles southwest of the school.

ERIC & DYLAN. Kaboom!

ERIC. Just enough fireworks to get the attention of the Jefferson County sheriff

DYLAN. ...and fire department.

ERIC & DYLAN. Jee-haaa!

ERIC. Eleven a.m.?

DYLAN. We're at the school.

ERIC. I park in the Senior Lot—

DYLAN. I, the Junior Lot.

ERIC. Positioned perfectly at the South door.

DYLAN. I, the Southwest door.

ERIC. Just in case someone survives the explosion of...

DYLAN. Two twenty-pound propane bombs.

ERIC. Eleven-ten a.m.?

DYLAN. We enter the cafeteria...

ERIC. Never being noticed...

DYLAN. And place the two bombs among the hundreds of backpacks...

ERIC. Never being noticed.

ERIC. At eleven-fifteen, over five hundred students have now entered the cafeteria.

DYLAN. Little do they know...

ERIC. In two minutes, the bombs are wired to explode.

DYLAN. Just in time to get one fork full in.

ERIC. Then back to our cars

DYLAN. Pick up our guns

ERIC. And wait.
DYLAN. And wait.
ERIC. Eleven-seventeen.
DYLAN. Eleven-seventeen

(ERIC and DYLAN celebrate and run around, as the company takes positions for "The Parents.")

DYLAN. Think of their faces...
ERIC. The ones on fire, screaming for help...
DYLAN. The world noticing our little high school, engulfed in flames.
ERIC. The power we'll have...
DYLAN. The fame we'll have.
ERIC. Like gods, man, like fucking gods.
DYLAN. The world will be studying our every move.
ERIC. Our journals...
DYLAN. Our lives...
ERIC. Our parents.

THE PARENTS

(Lights come up on ERIC's and DYLAN's parents, situated as in the dinner scene. ERIC and DYLAN circle them during the following...)

ACTOR (Perfect). I have been asked by the family of Eric Harris to assist them through the aftermath of the tragic events at Columbine High School. I am requesting that the media respect their privacy and refrain from contacting any family member.

ERIC. Don't blame my family, they had no clue. They're the best fucking parents I have ever known.

ACTOR. We want to express our heartfelt sympathy to the families of all of the victims for this senseless tragedy.

ERIC. Good wombs hath born bad sons.

ACTOR. Please say prayers for everyone touched by these horrible events.

ERIC. My dad is great. I wish I was a fucking sociopath so I didn't have any remorse, but I do.

ACTOR (Perfect). The Harris family is devastated by the deaths of the Columbine High students and is mourning the death of their youngest son, Eric.

ERIC. There is nothing you could've done to prevent what will happen.

(Lights focus on the Klebold dinner table.)

ACTOR (Prep). From a *New York Times* interview with the parents of Dylan Klebold…

DYLAN'S FATHER (AP). When we first heard about the shootings, it didn't occur to us that Dylan could be to blame.

DYLAN. Why would it?

DYLAN'S MOTHER (Faith). When we found out, we ran for our lives…went into hiding. We couldn't even grieve for our child.

DYLAN. There's nothing you could have done.

DYLAN'S FATHER. He was hopeless. We didn't realize it until after the end.

DYLAN. Hopeless?

DYLAN'S FATHER. A week before we were picking out dorm rooms for college…

DYLAN. I didn't want you to know. What could you have done?

DYLAN'S FATHER. The next is like a hurricane...a rain of fire...

DYLAN. What could I have said?

DYLAN'S MOTHER. Dylan didn't do this because of the way he was raised. He did it in contradiction to the way he was raised.

DYLAN. They gave me my fucking life. It's up to me what I do with it.

DYLAN'S MOTHER. Somebody said, "I forgive you for what you've done." I haven't done anything for which I need forgiveness.

DYLAN. No. You didn't do anything.

DYLAN'S FATHER. Our lawyer said, "Dylan isn't here anymore for people to hate. People are going to hate you."

DYLAN. This is going to tear them apart.

DYLAN'S MOTHER (Faith). I think he suffered horribly before he died.

DYLAN. Mom...

DYLAN'S MOTHER. For not seeing that, I will never forgive myself.

DYLAN. They'll never forget it.

ERIC *(yanks DYLAN out of the dinner scenes)*. And neither will those who survive. You'll never forget what you put us through. *(To the masses.)* GODDAMNIT! DO YOU HEAR ME? Do not blame anyone but me and V!

DYLAN. This was our choice. Our decision.

ERIC. More rage.

DYLAN. More rage...

ERIC. Keep building on it.

DYLAN. God, I can't wait till I can fucking kill you people.

(They pick up their guns.)

ERIC. You all better hide in your fucking houses because I'm coming for EVERYONE soon, and I WILL be armed to the fucking teeth and I WILL shoot to kill and I WILL fucking KILL EVERYTHING!

(The clock projects 11:17.)

DYLAN. GO!
ERIC. GO!
DYLAN & ERIC. GO!

(Blackout. Three horrific gunshots are heard.)

911

(The following sequence is projected onto the slate as a recording of the actual call is heard.)

DISPATCHER. Jefferson County 911…
TEACHER. Yes, I'm a teacher at Columbine High School and there is a student here with a gun. He just shot out a window. I believe, um, um.
DISPATCHER. Columbine High School?
TEACHER. I don't know what's in my shoulder. If it was just some glass or what.
DISPATCHER. Has anyone been injured, ma'am?
TEACHER. I am, yes…yes!

DISPATCHER. Okay.

TEACHER. Yes!...and the school is in a panic, and I'm in the library. I've got...students down. *(To students.)* Under the table kids, heads under the table! Kids are screaming, and the teachers are trying to take control of things. We need police here...

DISPATCHER. Okay, we're getting them there.

TEACHER. Can you please hurry!

DISPATCHER. Who is the student, ma'am?

TEACHER. I do not know who the student is.

DISPATCHER. Okay.

TEACHER. I saw a student outside... I was in the hall... Oh Dear God...Okay, I was on hall duty. I saw a gun and said, "What's going on out there?" And this kid said "Oh, it's probably a video production, probably a joke." *(Talking to student.)* I said "Well, I don't think that's a good idea," and...I went walking outside...to see what was going on. He turned the gun straight at us and shot and...oh my God, the window went out. And the kid standing there with me, I think he got hit.

DISPATCHER. Okay.

TEACHER. I have something in my shoulder.

DISPATCHER. Okay, we got help on the way, ma'am. *(Large bang.)*

TEACHER. Okay... Oh God!

DISPATCHER. Stay on the line with me *(Large bang.)*

TEACHER. Oh God! Kids, stay down.

DISPATCHER. Do we know where he's at?

TEACHER. I'm sorry

DISPATCHER. Do we know where he's at?

TEACHER. Okay...I'm in the library. He's upstairs. He's right outside here.

DISPATCHER. Outside of the hall or outside—

TEACHER. In the hall

DISPATCHER. Okay.

TEACHER. There are alarms and things going off. Smoke... *(Yelling:)* My God, smoke is coming into this room.

DISPATCHER. Okay...I just want you to stay on the line with me. We need to know what's going on.

TEACHER. Okay. I am on the floor.

DISPATCHER. Okay, you've got the kids there?

TEACHER. In the library...and I've got every student IN THE LIBRARY ON THE FLOOR. *(To students.)* AND YOU GOTTA STAY ON THE FLOOR!

DISPATCHER. Is there any way you can lock the doors?

TEACHER. Um...smoke is coming in from out there, and... *(gunfire)* the gun is right outside the library door... Okay, I don't think I'm going to go out there.

DISPATCHER. Okay, you're at Columbine High School?

TEACHER. I've got three children.

DISPATCHER. Okay we've got it...

TEACHER. Okay...I'm...

DISPATCHER. Yes...

TEACHER. I'm going to go to the door to shut the door, Okay... I've got the kids on the floor, um...I got all the kids in the library on the...

DISPATCHER. We have paramedics, we have fire and police en route...Okay...sir?

TEACHER. Okay

DISPATCHER. Is there any way you can block the door, so no one can get in?

TEACHER. I...yes...I guess I can try to go, but I mean like he's right outside that door I'm afraid to go to that door

DISPATCHER. That's Okay.

TEACHER. That's where he is. I don't know. I said, "What...what has that kid got?" He was outside at the time. And...and...and...um. I was on hall duty. *(Explosion.)* Oh God... And he was going, he was like woo, hoo, woo hoo...

DISPATCHER. Mmm-hmm, I know

TEACHER. ...like getting shot off. I said, "What's going on out there?" ...said it's a cap gun, probably a video production. You know they do these videos

DISPATCHER. Right

TEACHER. That's not, you know, a play gun, a real gun, I was going out there to say, "No" and I went walk— *(Huge gunfire.)* Oh my God, oh my God, that was really close.

DISPATCHER. Okay *(Huge gunfire.)*

(Lights up on DYLAN and ERIC, dressed in trench coats and gear.)

ERIC. Get up!

TEACHER *(whispers)*. Oh God...I hear him. I hear him. I think he's in here ... *(Two gunshots.)*

DYLAN. Get up.

DISPATCHER. What's your name, ma'am?

TEACHER *(whispers)*. My name is Patty.

ERIC & DYLAN. All the jocks stand up!

DISPATCHER. Patty?

TEACHER *(whispers)*. He just told everyone to get up now... He's in the library. He's shooting kids...

THE LIBRARY

(During this scene, the actors sit among tables and chairs recounting the events of April 20, 1999. ERIC and DYLAN face the chalk slate, their backs to the audience. They never directly interact with the other actors, even in real time. The gunshots and explosions are achieved by ERIC and DYLAN slamming their hands against the slate. They do not use guns in this scene. The actors should resist emotion and ultimately are frustrated that they have to participate in this scene. The retelling never gets indulgent, emotional, or anything like a recreation.)

ERIC. Everyone wearing a white hat, stand up!

ACTOR (Jock). Nobody stood up.

ERIC. Fine, I start shooting.

ACTOR (AP). They moved in front of the librarian's desk. I could have reached out and touched their legs.

DYLAN. Everyone's afraid, look at all the scared people under the tables.

ERIC. If you're wearing a hat or have a sports emblem on your shirt, you're dead.

ACTOR (Jock). That Saturday I got my hair cut, otherwise I would have been wearing my hat.

ACTOR (Faith). They made their way down toward the windows. They picked out a boy who wore glasses.

ERIC. You think those glasses are cool. Geek.

DYLAN. You think you're cool? Pathetic, fat boy!

ACTOR (Faith). Kyle Velasquez was sitting at a computer desk. He was the only one not hiding. *(DYLAN shoots.)* Kyle slumped over his monitor.

ERIC. This is for all the bullshit Columbine put us through.

DYLAN. Now I finally get my revenge.

ACTOR (Rebel). They put down their backpacks on a computer table...

DYLAN. The pigs are here.

ACTOR (Rebel). ...and crossed to the windows. They both fired over and over.

(DYLAN and ERIC simultaneously fire twice.)

ERIC. God, this is so much fun. I've waited my whole life for this.

DYLAN. Anyone with a white hat, stand up or I'll shoot everyone.

(All the male ACTORS slowly "remove their hats" from an impulsive memory rather than a recreation.)

ACTOR (Prep). Makai Hall, Patrick Ireland and I were all hiding together under a table. We were all wearing hats.

ACTOR (Jock). I hid my hat. And then Dan started to stand up. I grabbed his shoulder whispered not to move.

ACTOR (Prep). I wanted him not to shoot everyone under the table. I knew Dylan over the years. I looked him directly in the eye, hoping he might—

DYLAN *(raises his gun)*. Today is your day to die. *(DYLAN shoots.)*

ACTOR (Prep). Makai and I both were hit with buckshot. His leg was gushing blood. Patrick tried to stop the bleeding with his hands—

ACTOR (Jock). —But Makai warded off any help.

ACTOR (Prep). Then Patrick raised his head high enough above the table… *(DYLAN shoots.)* He dropped after being hit twice in the head.

ACTOR (Faith). I was hiding under a computer table in a little cubicle. Kacey was in the one next to me.

ACTOR (Rebel). There was a boy named Steven Curnow next to me. *(Looks R.)* On the other side was Amanda.

ACTOR (Faith). He bent down right next to the chair I had been sitting in…

ACTOR (Rebel). I turned around, plugged my ears and shrugged my shoulders. *(ERIC fires.)* Steven died.

ACTOR (Faith). The sound was deafening.

(ERIC turns and points a gun and fires.)

ACTOR (Rebel). With a 12-gauge shotgun at close range, he had shot a three-inch hole in my shoulder. I was moaning.

ERIC. Quit your bitching.

ACTOR (Rebel). I thought I was going to get shot again… so I leaned over the cubicle and pretended to be dead.

ACTOR (Faith). He moved away.

ERIC. Don't worry you're all gonna be dead in a couple of minutes.

ACTORS. Why are you doing this?

ERIC. This is payback.

DYLAN. This is what you deserve.

ERIC. Who's going to be next in line to die?

ACTOR (Perfect). I was out in the open. There was no room under any of the nearby tables.

ACTOR (Rebel). One of them walked past Cassie and I. We were shaking. Then Cassie started praying out loud.

ACTOR (Perfect). She kept saying, "Dear God, Dear God, why is this happening? I just want to go home."

ACTOR (Rebel). I immediately buried my head in the floor as he passed. He banged on the table.

ERIC *(knocks on the chalk slate)*. Peekaboo.

ACTOR (Rebel). He took a closer look at Cassie, as she put her hands over her head. *(ERIC shoots.)* He shot her point blank in the temple. Cassie looked at me, bewildered, then slumped to the floor and died.

ACTOR (Perfect). I never took my eyes off of him. He was so close to me. He looked disoriented. I saw blood streaming down his face.

ERIC. I hit myself in the face.

DYLAN. Cool.

ACTOR (Perfect). He was on the balls of his feet. He swung his gun back and forth in front of us. Then it pointed directly at me. He said:

(Lights isolate ERIC and ACTOR PLAYING PERFECT. This moment goes into real time.)

ERIC. Do you want to die?

ACTOR (Perfect). "No."

ERIC. Do you want to die?

ACTOR (Perfect). "No."

ERIC. Do you want to die?

ACTOR (Perfect) *(barely audible)*. No.

ERIC. Everyone's going to die.

DYLAN. Shoot her.
ERIC. No, we're gonna blow up the whole school anyway.

(Lights restore.)

ACTOR (Perfect). Then he got distracted. I heard Isaiah
    say "mom" and something about "home"
ERIC. Oh look, it's a nigger.
ACTOR (Jock). Matt Kechter and I were under the same
    table as Isaiah.
DYLAN. There's a nigger over here!
ACTOR (Jock). Isaiah tried to back up under the table.
    Dylan grabbed him, struggling to pull him out.

(ERIC shoots.)

DYLAN *(looks to his hands and on his body)*. Look at this
    black kid's brains! Awesome, man!
ERIC. Man, I never knew nigger brain could fly that far.

(DYLAN shoots.)

ACTOR (Jock). In a fury of shooting, Matt fell dead. I was
    covered in his blood, so I rolled over immediately, and
    played dead.
ERIC. Is he dead? I wanna know if that nigger's dead.
DYLAN. Yeah, he's dead.
ACTOR (Prep). They whooped in celebration.
ERIC. WHOO-HOO.
ACTOR (Prep). They were having the time of their lives.
DYLAN. I can't believe I did that. *(Pause.)* Cool.

ERIC. Who's ready to die next? *(ERIC gestures as if throwing something.)*

ACTOR (Prep). It was a small CO_2 cartridge. It was sizzling under the table. I saw it. I grabbed it. I threw it.

(DYLAN and ERIC create an explosion by banging on the board.)

ACTOR (AP). Then he did the craziest thing. He started jumping on bookshelves, shaking them back and forth. Cursing wildly. Firing his gun, shooting books. *(ERIC walks away from the group. He kneels behind a table, unseen.)* Then he disappeared. I couldn't see him. He was behind the bookshelves—alone.

(DYLAN shoots.)

ACTOR (Faith). He had blasted the display cabinet to pieces. It was full of sports trophies. Then he spotted Mark Kintgen. I knew it was Mark because his cerebral palsy made him move slow. *(DYLAN fires twice.)* Two 9mm bullets: one to his neck, one into his head.

(DYLAN begins a repeated firing of his gun, slowly increasing in speed.)

ACTOR (Perfect). It was me, Lauren, Valeen, Lisa and Jeanna, cramped under one table.

ACTOR (Faith). He wouldn't stop shooting. Shooting.

(Company shudders with each shot.)

ACTOR (Perfect). In that moment all you could do is pray that they won't shoot you. Pray that you won't die.

DYLAN *(rages)*. AHHHHHH!!! *(DYLAN stops.)*

ACTOR (Perfect). Lauren was dead.

ACTOR (Faith). Dylan would pass papers to me in government class. We used to talk about homework.

DYLAN *(rests his head against the chalk slate)*. Pathetic.

ACTOR (Faith). Valeen leaned over to me and said...

ACTOR (Rebel). You guys, I'm bleeding.

ACTOR (Faith). He turned to her.

(Lights isolate DYLAN and the ACTOR PLAYING REBEL. This moment goes into real time.)

ACTOR (Rebel) *(whispers)*. Oh my God... Oh my God...

(DYLAN shoots a single shot.)

DYLAN. God! Do you believe in God?

ACTOR (Rebel). Yes.

DYLAN. Why?

ACTOR (Rebel). That was the way my mom and dad had raised me.

(DYLAN walks away and joins ERIC. Lights restore.)

ACTOR (Perfect). I was alone under a table. I asked John Tomlin if I could join him under his. He motioned me over. I started talking to him. He calmly put his hand over my mouth and said, "Shhh, shhh." Then we saw the legs coming. He held my hand.

ERIC. Watch my back. *(ERIC fires.)*

ACTOR (Perfect). We were hit. John crawled out from table to get away. *(DYLAN fires. ERIC turns around and fires immediately.)* He shot him. I felt his legs shake against mine.

ERIC. Are you still breathing?

ACTOR (Perfect). I didn't know who he was asking so I just closed my eyes. I just blacked out.

(ERIC fires.)

DYLAN. Let's go kill some cops.

ERIC. I need to reload. Where's the bag?

ACTOR (Faith). They were moving around my table. I heard something about "using the shells." Then…

(Lights isolate. DYLAN points his gun in her face. He holds it there for fifteen seconds. This moment goes into real time.)

ACTOR (Faith). He walked away.

(Lights restore.)

ERIC. Who is under the table? Identify yourself!

(Lights isolate DYLAN and ACTOR PLAYING AP. This moment goes into real time.)

ACTOR (AP). I said "It's me, John."

DYLAN. John Savage?

ACTOR (AP). Yes.

DYLAN. Hi.

ACTOR (AP). Hi, Dylan. What are you doing?

DYLAN. Oh, killing people.

ACTOR (AP). Are you going to kill me?

DYLAN *(looks to ERIC. Pause)*. No, dude. Just run. Just get out of here.

(Lights restore.)

ACTOR (AP). I remember if he said "yes," I would have said, "Then make it quick. Just put a bullet in my head and get it over with." But he let me go.

ACTOR (Prep). We were about one desk over and one back from Daniel Mauser. Brittany and I were getting really worried. I tried to block her with my shoulder and back. All I could think of was in *Lethal Weapon*, or one of those action movies, they said it's hard to kill somebody if they're looking you in the eyes. *(ERIC fires.)* But then he shot Daniel, who tried to push chairs at him and tried to grab his legs...anything to make him stop. But he only shot again, and again. *(ERIC fires.)* Then Daniel was still.

DYLAN *(laughing)*. Did he try to grab you?

ACTOR (Perfect). Corey gripped my hand. "Stay tight the cops will come," he said. Jenny was on the other side of us. I looked up and right into his eyes. *(ERIC and DYLAN fire.)* Jenny screamed in pain. Corey's back was covered in blood. His head was... *(Looks at her hands.)*

DYLAN. Hey, you know I always wanted to kill somebody with a knife. There's more blood with a knife.

ACTOR (Perfect). I closed my eyes. I played dead. I was playing dead when I felt him...his body stopped moving...breathing.

DYLAN. You all better get up and leave. We're gonna blow up this library. *(ERIC moves around upstage. DYLAN stops and notices the JOCK.)* Well, look what we have here.

(Lights isolate DYLAN and ACTOR PLAYING JOCK. This moment goes into real time.)

ERIC. What?

DYLAN. Just some fat fuck. *(DYLAN slowly points the gun at JOCK.)* Are you a jock?

ACTOR (Jock). No.

DYLAN. Well, that's good. We don't like jocks. *(DYLAN looks closer into his face.)* Let me see your face. *(Pause.)* Give me one good reason why I shouldn't kill you?

ACTOR (Jock). I don't wanna get into trouble. I don't want to get into trouble.

DYLAN. Trouble? You don't know what fucking trouble is.

ACTOR (Jock). That's not what I meant. I mean I don't have a problem with you guys, I never will and I never did.

DYLAN. I'm going to let this fat fuck live, you can have him if you want to. *(Lowering his gun. Lights restore.)* Let's go to the Commons.

ERIC. We have one more thing to do.

(Blackout.)

GOODBYE

(The following is heard. It is the audio from the boys' goodbye video.)

ERIC. Say it now.

DYLAN. Hey, Mom. Gotta go. It's about half an hour before our little judgment day. I just wanted to apologize to you guys for any crap this might instigate as far as... *(camera jiggles; this is inaudible)* or something. Just know I'm going to a better place than here. I didn't like life too much and I know I'll be happier wherever the fuck I go. So I'm gone. Goodbye. Reb...

(Lights slowly come up on DYLAN and ERIC, walking slowly to the center of the chalk slate. ERIC carries the shotgun, DYLAN, the TEC-9.)

ERIC. Yeah... Everyone I love I'm really sorry about all this. I know my mom and dad will be just like just fucking shocked beyond belief. I'm sorry all right. I can't help it.

DYLAN. We did what we had to do.

ERIC. Morris, Nate, if you guys live I want you guys to have whatever you want from my room and the computer room.

DYLAN. Yeah, take whatever you want of mine.

ERIC *(beat)*. That's it. *(Long beat.)* Sorry. Goodbye.

(ERIC slowly puts the shotgun into his mouth. DYLAN slowly raises the TEC-9 to his left temple.)

DYLAN. Goodbye.

(Blackout as two shots are heard.)

AFTERMATH

(Lights on PREP and REBEL, sitting.)

ACTOR (Rebel). They were bringing the kids to Leawood Elementary as they were rescued from the school. At the beginning, we were looking for John but he was just never showing up. I was getting envious of parents who were finding their kids, or those that kept screaming out their kids' names. I had no enthusiasm to jump up and look for him. We just sat in the back of the room.

ACTOR (Prep). You don't want to jump to any conclusions. So, as every bus arrived, you're hoping that your kid is on that bus.

ACTOR (Rebel). Then the sheriff came around to us and said most of the kids that are dead are in the library. He always went to the library. That's where he did his homework. I felt like I was going to pass out. I told the officer, "I have to go home. I have to be with my other children." When I got there, I went up to the shower and prayed with every part of my being. "Lord, thank you for the sixteen years I've had with John. Let his death not be in vain."

(Lights to FAITH and JOCK.)

ACTOR (Faith). The police weren't giving us any information, so we finally gave up and went home—we don't live far from the school. I couldn't sleep. I was laying there thinking, "Cassie's over the fence a hundred yards away and they won't let us get to her."

ACTOR (Jock). It was three a.m. We decided to walk to the school. We ran into a police officer and said we just wanted to know what the truth is, if there is anyone left alive in there. He paused and said, "No." I said "Thanks we appreciate your honesty."

ACTOR (Faith). It was two a.m. Thursday when we finally got the official call.

ACTOR (Jock). They were going to start the autopsy that afternoon, but I said we wanted to see her right away... before you do anything to her. We heard she was shot in the head so we expected the worst. I went in first...and surprisingly, she looked pretty good, considering. It was our Cassie. I kissed her toes, her cheek. She was cold.

(Lights on AP.)

ACTOR (AP). That night, one of the other pastors said, "We better go back to our churches. People will be coming soon." A background theme kept playing in my head, "Who were the dumb parents of this mess?" As I was handing out Eucharist, "Body of Christ" *(with PERFECT: Amen)* "Body of Christ" someone says *(with FAITH: "Klebold")* I say "Body of Christ" I get *(with the OTHER ACTORS "Klebold.")* I suddenly recognize the name. I said, "If they need me, have them call." On Thursday, I get the call, "Would you do a funeral for my son?" When I arrive, I met Sue. She was shaking. I held her, but could feel...nothing. Then, there was Dylan... lying in a casket, around his neck was this ring of

Beanie Babies. He had grown since I last saw him. I stand there thinking, "How do I commend this boy—this mass murderer—to heaven?" Tom says, "How could this happen? Who the hell gave my son a gun?" The mother says, "How could he be anti-Semitic, he is half Jewish." All I could say was that a parent's love is as faithful as God's. We die many times and we experience many forms of grief but love…it never fails.

ACTORS. 15.

ACTOR (Prep). I was in Florida when a friend called asking me to build fifteen crosses for the victims at Columbine. When we got there, there were all kinds of people sitting there on the hill behind the school. So me and my son, we went up there but I remember him saying, "Dad, don't put those crosses up for those two. You're going to get in a lot of trouble." But I wanted to honor the request.

ACTORS. 13.

ACTOR (Jock). I couldn't believe it. I contacted the park service to take those two crosses down, and when they stayed, I took care of it myself. You don't build a monument to Adolf Hitler and put it in a Holocaust museum—and it's not going to happen here.

ACTORS. 15.

ACTOR (Faith). We have a prayer garden in the back of our church, and our pastor was talking about planting trees for the victims. Before the issue was settled, the nursery brought over fifteen trees. We thought it through and decided to plant fifteen.

ACTORS. 13.

ACTOR (Rebel). That Sunday fifty picketers showed up carrying signs and as services continued indoors, a few of the victim's parents sawed down the two trees that stood at the pinnacle of the semicircle. I remember one of them saying, "I was getting all my anger out on that tree. It felt good."

(Projected: "One Year Later."

Lights to JOCK.)

ACTOR (Jock). Well honestly? We're tired. Tired of picking up the newspapers or turning on the TV and hearing about the shootings. It seems like every move we make is under a microscope. Columbine is no different from any other high school in the United States. We just want to move on.

(Lights to REBEL.)

ACTOR (Rebel). There is no such thing as closure. It's our kids, and we don't want to put them behind us. But everyone wants to know why it happened, if it could have been prevented, and, most important, what can we do right this minute to keep it from happening again?

(Projected: "Three Years Later.")

ACTOR (Faith). What I don't understand is that they heard the 911 call...for twenty minutes they knew exactly where Klebold and Harris were...for twenty minutes they listened to them murdering children, and they just stood outside. If someone had radioed that a cop was down, they would have stormed the building. There isn't one parent who wouldn't have gone in that school that day.

ACTOR (AP). We did what we did. We don't make any apologies for it. We have communicated extensively with the families at every turn. The fact is we don't have anyone to prosecute for these murders, so this community has turned to attack the very people who have tried to help them.

(Projected: "Five Years Later.")

ACTOR (Prep). It is a proven fact that the police had fifteen points of contact with Harris and Klebold prior to the shootings. But those reports, the boys' videos and other evidence, have been kept from us, or in some cases, destroyed. The public needs access to the facts—not just bits and pieces of the story, but the whole ugly package. That hasn't happened with Columbine.

(Projected: "Seven Years Later.")

ACTOR (Perfect). I don't know what to say. I think this community is permanently wounded. Ever since that day we've been obsessed with moving on, or getting back... so we've gone to gun control...

ACTOR (Prep). the music...

ACTOR (AP). computer games...

ACTOR (Jock). the school...

ACTOR (Faith). the police...

ACTOR (Rebel). the parents...

ACTOR (Perfect). ...looking for someone to blame. But we always find ourselves back where we started asking the same question...

ACTORS. Why?

(Lights come up on full stage. ACTOR PLAYING JOCK stands center.

Projected: "Today.")

ACTOR (Jock). It's been a few years now, and just the other day, I was driving past the school and I stopped at the stoplight and I looked at the kids yelling at each other on the sidewalk, guys on the court, the normalness of it all. And then I saw a kid get out his car...he had on baggy pants, a lot of chains, combat boots and a long black trench coat. My God! I had to pull off the side of the road. Now, what was in my head, must have been in everyone's head from that day until now...like that look, those clothes meant "evil." Evil was present. But Christ, how the hell would I know that kid is evil unless I actually talk to him? *(Beat.)* So how do I think differently about someone? For days after yeah, we all treated each other differently, but time passes and we still make judgments, call people shit, and continue on, just as before. Even after living through your friends dying and those sounds of gunblasts and the fear of walking down those halls again...all of that. Who knows? Maybe I have changed, a little. For the moment I'm different? But is that enough?

(The actors, lead by the ACTORS PLAYING DYLAN and ERIC, write the victims' names on the slate. When finished, they turn to the audience.)

ACTORS. Thank you. Good night.

(The actors exit. The lights fade, save for the illuminated chalkboard memorial.)

END OF PLAY

Production Notes

Staging *columbinus* is a challenging task. We were heavily influenced by the theatrical styles of Bertolt Brecht and Peter Brook: minimalist theatre with a strong awareness of the actor, the space, and the reason why the artists are doing the play. The production should be simple and honest. There should be no attempt to create sets and costumes for each location, transitions between scenes, or mask anything offstage. The scenes run like a surreal river, each flowing into the next. Therefore, sound and lighting are major elements, constantly redefining the space into new locations.

The projections and some of the technical elements are a challenging but critical undertaking. The technical sequences like **I.M.** or **911** should never be spoken by the actors. It robs the audience of the real experiences intended: the silent communication of teenagers, and the harsh reality of events of April 20, 1999. Although we explored the use of live video feed in several moments, **Work** was the only scene where it was successfully employed. The use of live video creates the problem of split focus (moments in which the audience isn't sure whether to watch the actors or the video), so we encourage you to explore its use long before you reach **Tech**. Remember, the story needs to be told clearly, simply, and as humanly as possible. After four years and three productions, we discovered: less is more.

The chalkboard memorial is one of the most powerful moments in the production. As explained in the **Aftermath**, there is much controversy about whether or not to include the names of Dylan and Eric among the victims of the Columbine tragedy. We did not. We felt the play focuses so heavily on Dylan and Eric that it was a more fitting memorial to end by remembering the victims.

We'll mention the obvious: there should be absolutely no cutting, censoring, or editing of *columbinus*. First of all, it's illegal. Secondly, by producing the play, you have a responsibility to the people who shared their stories with us. The world of adolescents and the Columbine tragedy are filled with the beautiful and the disturbing. They need to exist as they were discovered, otherwise it is not truthful.

Engaging the actors/designers in the reason why they are doing the show should be at the heart of every production of *columbinus*. We encourage everyone involved in the production to research the events of the Columbine Shootings. We also encourage the actors (provided they aren't teenagers themselves) to take some time to observe adolescents. Engage them in conversation (but do more listening than talking). You'll be amazed at what you hear.

— PJ Paparelli
February 1, 2007

DIRECTOR'S NOTES